بسم الله

الله

الحمد لله رب العالمين الرحيم

اهدنا الصراط المستقيم صراط الذين

غير المغضوب عليهم

Dear Iran,

We had so much still to show you,

Love,

Veena & Salman

10th - 24th Jan '97

MOHAMED AMIN · DUNCAN WILLETTS · BRENDAN FARROW

PAKISTAN

FROM MOUNTAINS TO SEA

Camerapix Publishers International
NAIROBI

First published 1994 by
Camerapix Publishers International,
P.O. Box 45048,
Nairobi, Kenya

© Camerapix 1994

ISBN 1 874041 25 3

This book was designed and produced by
Camerapix Publishers International,
P.O. Box 45048,
Nairobi, Kenya

Edited by Brian Tetley
Production Editor: Debbie Gaiger
Typeset: Kimberly Davis
Design: Craig Dodd

Printed in Hong Kong by South China Printing (1988) Limited.

Contents

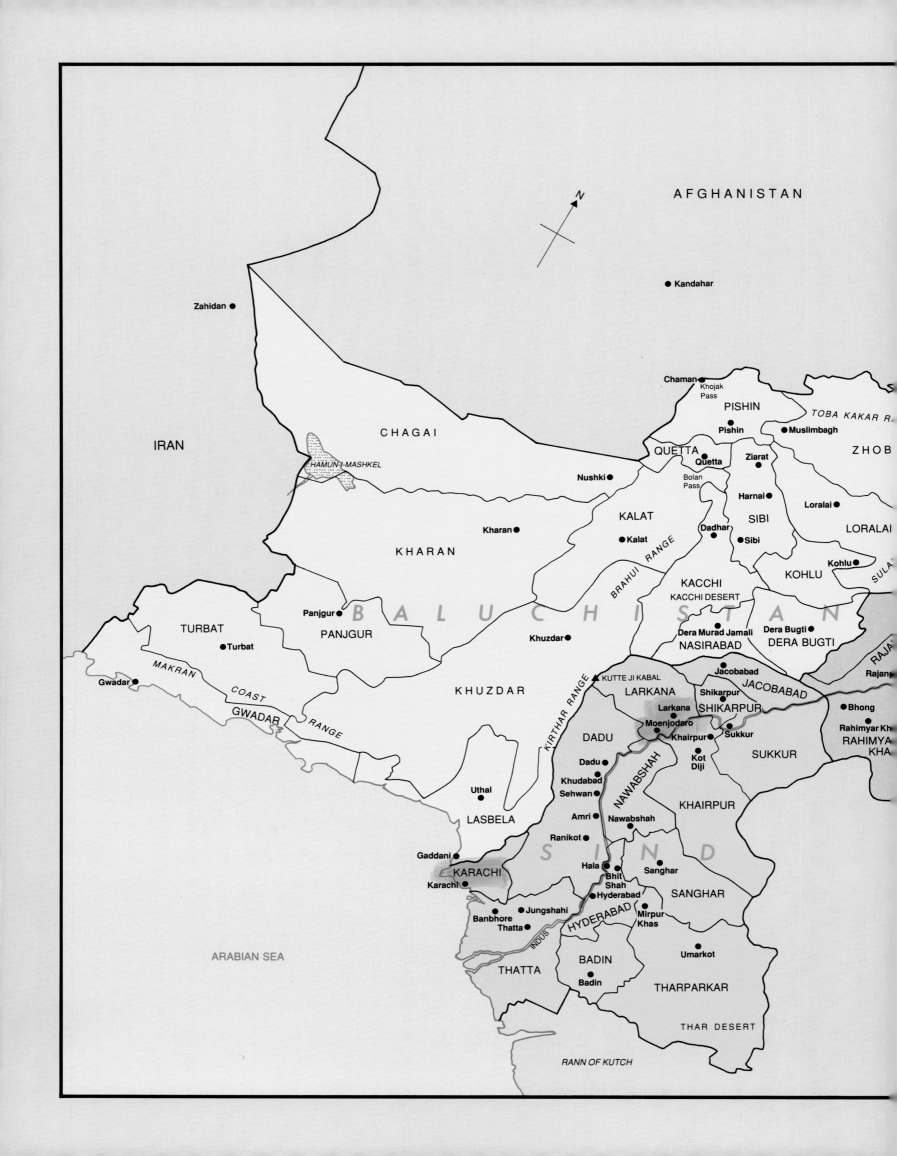

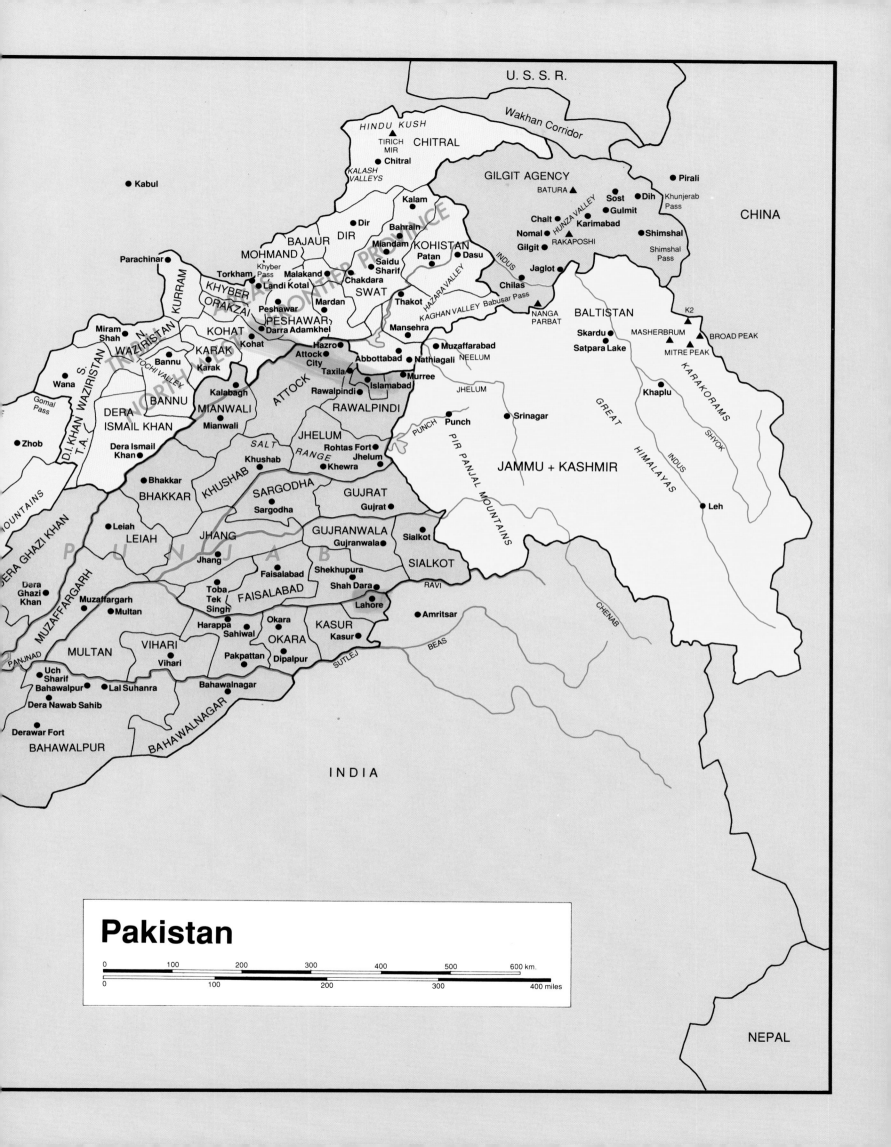

Pakistan

Introduction: A Portrait

'If you would see me
Look on me with love.'
— Legend on a Pakistani truck

Three great river valleys cut through the desert-steppes of the Old World: the Nile, the Tigris-Euphrates and the Indus. Each holds an unrivalled place in the world's history. Each was a cradle of civilization.

Everybody knows about the Egypt of the pharaohs, though few give much thought to the builders — practically slaves — of those landmark tombs, the pyramids. The Twin-River cities too — especially Ur and ancient Babylon — are well enough known, if only for their Hanging Gardens and ziggurats. But Pakistan — in the Indus valley, the easternmost of the three — is rarely classed with the other two; and almost never ranked equal.

There's an irony in this, especially in today's world with its emphasis on the importance of planned urban development and concern for the environment. For the ancient Indus Valley civilization centered on the twin cities of Harappa (in today's Pakistan province of Punjab) and Moenjodaro (in today's Sind) far excelled the others in many ways — most particularly in the importance attached to planning and environmental considerations. This extraordinary civil empire of precisely planned, elaborately organised, health and hygiene-conscious communities spread its meticulous influence across a distance of 1,610 kilometres, from the Iranian border to the foothills of the Himalaya, via the Gulf of Cambay in India: far further than its two contempories — ancient Egypt and the Twin-River cities — combined. To the celebrated British archaeologist Sir Mortimer Wheeler it was the 'the vastest experiment in civilization before the Roman Empire'. Two thousand years before — it should be noted. If only for this, Pakistan's is a pedigree without compare in South Asia.

But the Indus Valley's civilization is only one of the gems in Pakistan's store. An unsurpassed pageant of event and achievement went before and followed after — all of it staged in terrain that for drama and spectacular variety of scenery few countries can match. In Pakistan the superlatives are simply fact.

For altitude, numbers and density the chockablock mountains of Pakistan's north outrank those of every comparable area in the world.

At the same time, buried like jewels deep among these often impenetrable, ice-bound rock fastnesses are valleys of such natural perfection that they inspired the legends of Shangri-La — valleys that breathe only fresh, flower-fragrant clean air under ever-blue sun-bright skies, where crystal-clear waters fill the trees with an abundance of lush fruit, and men and women live in peace and contentment, the joy of life unsullied for those whom the gods have chosen to bless.

Yet further south in this same country, both to the east and across most of Baluchistan's western massif, lie stark and deadly deserts, salt lakes and barren plateaux that for aridity, searing heat, and literally lethal winds are among the earth's most feared.

And by contrast again, between these fierce deserts and in the lee of those forbidding northern mountains, lie immense and richly fertile plainlands which have generated such vast wealth that they have invited — and suffered through the ages — invasion from all the hill and mountain country about, especially the north-west.

This sometimes fatal fertility is here the gift of rain, there of the flow of five huge and wilful rivers which join forces one after another before

Above: Young girls enjoy the age-old game of blind man's bluff in the Sheikhupura park that Jahangir dedicated to his favourite antelope.

Opposite top left: Shimshal woman in the traditional hat of her mountainous region near the Chinese border.

Opposite top: Venerable Pathan elder with rifle.

Opposite left: Smiling but pensive girls in the traditional dress of Baluchistan.

Opposite: Sindhi street musician joins the celebrations for a newly-wed couple.

paying their single tribute to the Indus — the mighty waterway fabled in the orient and occident alike, which for more than 2,000 years gave the entire subcontinent its name.

This Indus and its tributaries are still the life-blood of Pakistan. Their waters hold — as they always did — the power of life and death over its people. Throughout known time their seemingly wanton abandonment of one bed in favour of another has made and broken farmers, villages and regional capitals without warning or by-your-leave. The Indus may well have drowned the mighty head city of the Indus Valley civilization, Moenjodaro. The sediments it today deposits in the ocean south of Karachi are still changing the profile of Pakistan's coast.

This awesome land of soaring mountains and rampaging rivers, of fiery deserts and bitter salt marshes, of verdant valleys and sparkling lakes, boasts also a superb seaboard — 800 kilometres of caves, coves, and golden beaches washed by the waters of the Arabian Sea. Incidentally, these nurture one of nature's rarest, most jealously guarded wonders, the cyclical rebirth of that improbable survivor of the dinosaur age — the giant turtle.

Pakistan has long been one of life's great havens. Especially for mankind. The north is among the few places where our immediate predecessors are known to have lived. There, too, man himself left an amazing number of his first stone tools, and then, 30,000 years ago, built one of his first crude shelters. The evidence remains.

This same land fostered greater growth yet. At Mehr Gahr, on a dried-up river bed near the Bolan Pass in Baluchistan, early man and his wife and children learned to govern the growth of plants and switched — for food and clothing — from the hazardous chances of the chase to the wiser husbandry of animals that would work for them. There, too, during their 5,000-year continuous occupation of the site they taught

Opposite: A 4,000-year-old well at Moenjodaro testifies to the sophistication and building skills of the Indus Civilization.

themselves those skills — of pottery, and later metalwork, always with decoration and ornament — that made civilization possible and wanted. Thus, Mehr Gahr represents many giant steps for mankind, all taken before the great civilizations of the Nile, the Tigris-Euphrates and the Indus had even begun.

All this is in the astonishing pedigree of the land now called Pakistan.

Later, much later, after the Indus Valley's heyday (2500-1800 BC) though still centuries before Rome, there began to emerge out of the hard passes of the north-west and, more rarely the east, that seemingly endless cavalcade of warlords and conquerors — Aryans from Central Asia; the first Buddhists; the Achaemenian Persians; Alexander the Great; the truly great Mauryans with their so admirable Ashoka; the Bactrian Greeks; Scythians; Parthians and Kushans; White Huns; Turks — the thunderbolts of history who preceded Mohamed bin Qasim. He came in the eighth century of our era, bringing the gift of the Prophet's message.

Islam was born in the previous century in Arabia, in the heart of that vast desert belt which Pakistan faces to the west. It is a religion which calls for profound yet simple faith, unites people where they speak to God — and so encourages a marvellous fraternity — imposes a sometimes stern code of conduct, and begets rich and vigorous cultures.

Bin Qasim's introduction of Islam to the Indus Valley was to have epic consequences. It is the single most important fact about Pakistan. For implicit in it was Pakistan itself. But not then. Not for more than a millennium.

After bin Qasim the invasions continued: Afghans, Mongols — Genghis Khan and Tamurlane in their own terrible and barbarously great persons — the fabulous Mughals, more Persians, the Sikhs, and finally the British. At one time or another they all coveted this arid but lush, stark yet wonderful, country. And all — for good or ill — left the marks of their passing upon it.

Frequently in the people. The distinct majorities of today's four provinces — Punjabis in Punjab, Sindhis in Sind, Baluchis in Baluchistan and Pathans in the North-West Frontier Province (NWFP) — are well known. So are much smaller communities like the Kafir Kalash — mainly, in their case, because they are non-Muslim in this predominantly Muslim state. But the diversity of races in Pakistan, especially in the north, is actually much greater — with origins ascribed by some to places as distant as China and modern Yugoslavia. Each has its own culture, dialect, even language. But all, with the exception of the Kalash — and the minority Christian, Hindu, and Parsis — are united in their creed, the Islamic faith and the institutions it inspires.

Pakistan's caravan, thousands of years long, thus carries riches few countries can match. The staggering order of Moenjodaro that attained sudden perfection so soon after the giant strides of Mehr Gahr, had risen, flourished and finally died 1,500 years before Aristotle's pupil, Alexander the Great, arrived to debate philosophy with the naked ascetics of Taxila's renowned University. And the Macedonian warlord was himself a 300-year-old memory when traders brought glass from Imperial Rome to New Taxila, which the Christian apostle Thomas, the Doubter, visited. Doubtless he wondered at the exhausted mule trains that staggered in, overloaded with purest silk from China, at the end of their frightful journey along the edge of the sheer, ice-bound ledges of the Roof of the World where one foot wrong in the blinding snow meant death. Their route through the Himalayan and Karakoram foothills took them past rocks engraved, two centuries before Christ, with edicts from a king enjoining tolerance and respect for the beliefs of others (the edicts survive), and their trade so flourished that it not only crowned virtually every Taxila hilltop with Buddhist monasteries and *stupas* (many now unearthed, many more still to be revealed), but also brought the Pakistan caravan many of its most remarkable treasures — among them the incomparable Fasting Buddha now in Lahore Museum.

Outstanding too, in this proud parade, are the achievements of the Mughals: their mosques, palaces, fortifications, monuments, and gardens, the way they used — especially under Shah Jahan — mosaics, glazes, frescos, *pietra dura*, calligraphy, and their exquisite miniature paintings. More recent triumphs are the colossal Tarbela Dam — once the largest earthfill dam in the world — and the Karakoram Highway, highest and surely the most incredible of roads, built where, almost 2,000 years earlier, those silk merchants went through the mountains to China, daily maintained and kept open by Pakistan's soldier-engineers.

Throughout Pakistan today's merchants still use mules — and camels and horses — led through the streets of twentieth-century Karachi in all the hurlyburly of the port-city's modern traffic, past the bazaars where traders, small farmers, and artisans display their produce, wares, and artefacts for hands on assessment and the all-important business (or is it a game?) of arguing the price.

It would be a mistake to see today's Pakistan as the inevitable conclusion of all that now glorious, now tragic past. No clear-cut path to development leads from Moenjodaro, Taxila, or even the Lahore of the Mughals to twentieth-century Islamabad. The territory was always too ruggedly diverse, the people too disparate for that. And yet a suprising number of the basic elements were there.

Unless modern rocketry and air warfare have destroyed all the tactical advantage of geographical features, this land's frontiers, for instance, could almost have been designed by nature to accommodate one nation: the north practically blocked off by the most forbidding concentration of mountains on earth, the south guarded by the sea, and the east barred by more terrible mountains and a vast desert. Only on the western side — from which by far the most numerous of invasions came — is the country relatively approachable; but even there only with difficulty.

What was needed was that the many peoples of this varied but homogeneous land should be drawn together and given a sense of national and spiritual unity. And this was done largely by the inspired labours of one man, Mohamed Ali Jinnah, Quaid-i-Azam, Great Leader, and thus founder of the country. Years before his final triumph he described the ground of this 'idea' of Pakistan as nobody else could.

'We are a nation with our own distinctive culture and civilization, language and literature, art and architecture, names and nomenclature, sense of values and proportion, legal laws and moral code, customs and

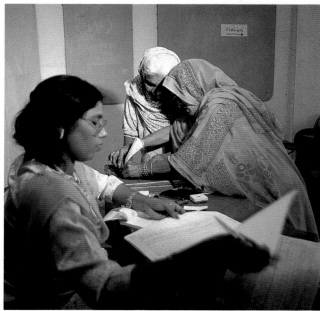

Top: Since Pakistan returned to democracy in the late 1980s, voters have turned out with partisan fervour to back the candidate of their choice.

Above: Women voters in the general elections.

calendar, history and tradition, aptitudes and ambitions; in short we have our own distinctive outlook on life and of life. By all canons of international law, we are a nation.'

To bring about the crucial change that made Pakistan's many people one, the Quaid and his followers had only to open those people's eyes.

Which is why Pakistan, with its unsurpassed heritage, nevertheless has a beginning in the twentieth century. The day that marked its debut on the world's stage was 14 August, 1947. It became an independent and sovereign state on this absolutely simple ground: that the millions of Muslims on the subcontinent were a nation, and must possess their own, sovereign, inviolable homeland.

It seems obvious and inevitable now; but at the time it was an astonishing triumph. No need to dwell on that oft-told story here; but one aspect of more recent history must be mentioned.

In only its fifth decade, Pakistan found itself neighbour to (and inevitably involved in) one of the nastiest and bloodiest of the twentieth-century's ideological struggles. In practical terms, this has meant bearing the brunt of what has been by far the largest of a scandalously refugee-ridden century's many immense problems in providing shelter and succour for millions of displaced people.

The Afghanistan conflict has not helped this young nation to realise its full economic potential, but — by accepting a burden much greater than those which countries richer and economically more developed continually shy away from — it has enabled it to practice what it preaches about the brotherhood of men.

Above: Pride and martial splendour of Pakistan Armed Forces Bands men.

These two instances reflect a character, an underlying strength in Pakistan, which might otherwise be lost to sight in the kaleidoscope of images that crowd into any portrait of this ever-old, ever-new land where laughing children go to school on the back of a clip-clop *tonga*, sharp-eyed Pathan soldiers guard a snow-stark frontier, dark-eyed boys with flashing smiles take buffalo to water in a Sind canal, nomads guide sheep across the corner of a Baluchistan desert, Makran coast fishermen wash their nets, and tourists revel in the Arabian Sea not far from Gaddani where, virtually bare-handed, men dismantle ocean-going freighters in perhaps the biggest breaker's yard in the world.

Everywhere crowds pray in the shrines of saints and scholars, poets and philosophers, or attend the Friday prayers in village mosques that can hold a few score and city mosques built for tens of thousands of faithful. Hindu and Sikh temples are to be seen, too, and Christian churches, and chaotic traffic flaunting here jewels of poetry and there humdrum platitudes.

Mountains as glorious as Rakaposhi preside over panoramas of incredible beauty and glaciers as stunning as Baltoro defy experienced mountaineers. Trekkers stand speechless before the glory of a Baltistan lake. Further south farmers irrigate fields, men mine salt and coal, city folk in *shalwar-kameez* enter offices and craftsmen seek perfection in the making of pottery, carpets, lacquer-work, and silk fabric.

And there are, of course, the snake-charmers whose cobras have heard it all before, the man with the bear that's too hot and tired for dancing except under (dangerous) provocation, gangs of green parrots screeching from banyan to banyan tree, and their macaw cousin wisely turning the

Opposite: Ornately-painted images of sacred Islamic places and religious calligraphy, together with intricate metal and woodwork, adorn a modern diesel truck in Gilgit, northern Pakistan.

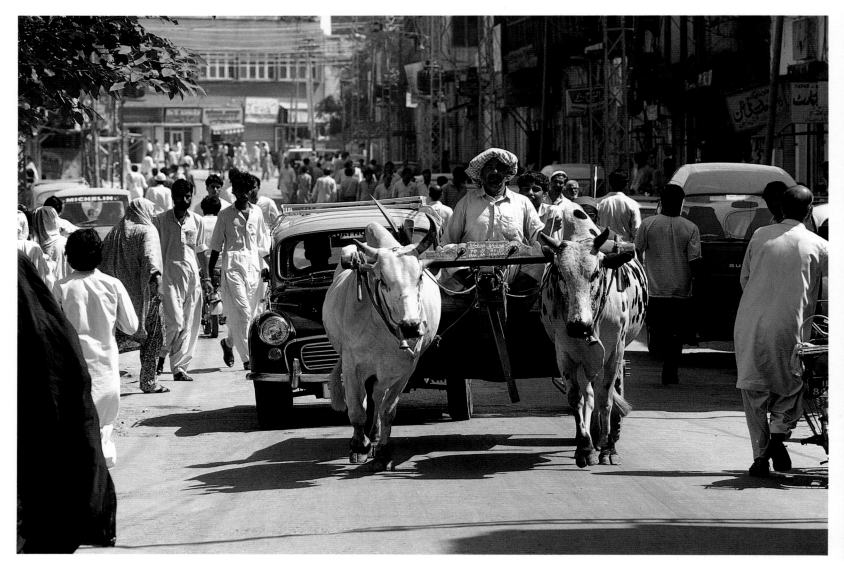

cards for the street fortune-teller whose skills have not much advantaged him or his bird.

In astonishing desert mirages, a posse of horsemen gallops suddenly out of nowhere along a silent railway line before striking off at an angle, apparently to nowhere else; a camel sways full of women, babies, chickens, pots, pans, and a kid-goat on its back while another, mesmerised by its rider's plaintive flute, dreams drowsily down the dried-up bed of a mountain river.

Dried-up or in spate, rivers are never far away in Pakistan — playful, pretty, and dangerous; bringers of life — and takers.

Pakistan is fabulously rich in its history, easy to love, and a wonder to behold . . . .

Above: Bullock cart in the crowded streets of Rawalpindi.

Overleaf: Space-age minarets of the multi-million dollar Faisal Mosque, Islamabad. The design of its central prayer hall was inspired by the tents of Arabia's bedouins.

Following pages: Faithful at worship inside Faisal Mosque which can accommodate 100,000 worshippers in its interior and courtyard.

'Live, my child . . .'
— Slogan on a Karachi truck

Immaculate in his tropical white uniform, the police sergeant was polite, friendly — and unmoved.

'But sir, no parking is allowed there. That is why . . . '

Those who've seen it will doubtless agree. There are few sights more pathetic than a car that has been hijacked on the twin prongs of a forklift disappearing round a bend.

'But we couldn't have been more than one minute. All my luggage, passport, money, clothes . . . .'

A big smile.

'Don't worry about that, sir. No problem. All will be all right. You must only pay the fine . . . .'

Pakistan's uncompromising attitude to parking offences — admirable so long as the vanishing car isn't your own — pays handsomely. It keeps both the main traffic arteries clear and the city's road department coffers constantly replenished.

But that first personal experience of its working was instructive at a deeper level. The luggage in the car wasn't all fastened, several things were loose, and everything came back untouched. Later experience proved it was no freak. Friendliness, politeness, firmness. And nothing stolen: an impressive introduction to a modern mega-city.

When the federal republic of Pakistan was born on 14 August, 1947, at the wish of the founder, Quaid-i-Azam Mohamed Ali Jinnah, the port city of Karachi, his birthplace, became its capital.

Karachi then counted 400,000 inhabitants at most. Forty years later, with the population already over seven million, 'ten million by the year 2000' was starting to look conservative. Twelve-, fifteen-million even, were being predicted.

Whatever the figure proves to be, Karachi has already secured a leading place in the league of the world's largest and fastest-growing cities. And even though construction of a fine, new, custom-built capital at Islamabad in the early 1960s deprived Karachi of that particular distinction its pre-eminence was in no way diminished. Formal status apart, Karachi then was, now is and — according to all the evidence — always will remain the first city of Pakistan.

It is an astonishing phenomenon.

Nearly 4,000 years after the Arabian Sea carried the last artefacts of the Indus Valley civilization to communities around the Arabian Gulf, that same sea brought to the land of the Indus the last of its innumerable invaders. Four thousand years! And in all that time, Karachi, this place from which the traders went and to which those last invaders came, is mentioned only twice in all the records of history.

The fact is striking because those records are busy with events in almost all modern Pakistan's other major cities. Karachi, it seems, never existed; or if it did, didn't matter. Yet today, like a babe born out of due time, Destiny's favourite, Karachi outdoes them all: outstrips in size, importance and economic strength every one of Pakistan's older, longer established towns and cities. Many of them are expanding vigorously, too; but it's Karachi alone, the kid brother, that has won a place among the great metropolitan cities of the world.

Those desperate for Karachi to have a past have suggested she is that Krokola from which Alexander the Great's admiral Nearchus sailed

Above: Medal-bedecked veteran of Pakistan's Armed Forces in ceremonial dress uniform.

Opposite: Marble terrace bathed in the warmth of a westering sun, Karachi's noblest monument — the mausoleum of Mohamed Ali Jinnah, Quaid-i-Azam, the Great Leader, founder of modern Pakistan — is classically Mughal in inspiration yet triumphantly modern in execution.

Previous pages: Oil jetty, storage tanks, and crowded berths of Karachi Port, one of the fastest growing shipping centres in the world.

34

westwards in 324 BC — in the closing stages of the Macedonian warlord's epic excursion into Asia. It may be so. More reliably, however, the great bay about which the modern city has grown is reckoned to be the one that Pliny and Ptolemy described when they sailed the region nearly 500 years after Alexander left.

But between them and a British navy survey early in the nineteenth century — again silence.

At the time of the British survey, Karachi was a small group of fishing villages on the mainland and adjacent islands. A few years later, in 1839, another British navy vessel — the young Queen Victoria's frigate *Wellesley* — fired a few broadsides and then, without a battle, accepted the surrender of the fort on the headland known as Manora.

It was the bay that interested the British. The situation made it perfect for development as a port that could rapidly become pivotal for trade and communications between the seat of Empire and the fabulous subcontinent that they prized above all other regions of the earth.

In his oft-quoted 1843 exclamation Sir Charles Napier, first British Governor of the Sind, prophesied that the seaport he addressed would become the glory of the East. 'Would that I could come again to see you in your grandeur!' he sighed.

It was this Napier who then shifted the status of 'capital', of the territory called Sind, from Hyderabad to Karachi, a move that today seems obviously right. At that time, however, it can have seemed so to very few. Hyderabad is one of the oldest cities on the subcontinent, possessed of a pre-Islamic pedigree and, for good measure, an impressive fort more than four square kilometres in area. But Karachi at the time was drab indeed.

In the year of Napier's prediction, Karachi counted some 9,000 Hindu and 5,000 Muslim inhabitants. They lived in a walled town, in a number of villages established along the banks of the muddy Lyari river and on nearby islands. Such community as these various groupings possessed came either from the river they all lived by — and which periodically disgorged huge quantities of its detritus in the great bay — or from the sea channel that wound a turbid way through the mangrove-entangled, swine-infested mud banks, and so strung the offshore islands together.

Karachi town had two gates: one, called *Karadar* (Salt Water gate), facing the sea; the other, *Mithadar* (Sweet Water gate) looking to the river. The names — though not the gates — survive: Karadar attached to a locality which has unique significance not just for Pakistan, but for all the history of the twentieth century.

It was in Karadar on 25 December, 1876 — the official, but not undisputed date — that Mohamed Ali Jinnah was born. He was to become Quaid-i-Azam — the Great Leader — architect of Muslim independence in the subcontinent, maker of Pakistan, and father of all its people. If ever a single man, directly through his own outstanding gifts of mind and character, immediately altered the course of history it was the Quaid. The proudest of all Karachi's claims to a unique status in the country that he created is this: to have been his birthplace, been home to his upbringing and early education, and to hold, in its greatest monument, his mortal remains. Karachi is the Quaid's city. But this anticipates.

Above: Portrait of the father of Pakistan, Mohamed Ali Jinnah, observes meticulously the remarkable acuity and single-mindedness which enabled Jinnah, virtually single-handed, to turn the tide of history and give reality to an independent Muslim homeland on the subcontinent.

Above: Marble plaque in Karachi's Newnham Street marks the room where the Quaid-i-Azam, Mohamed Ali Jinnah, was born on 25 December, 1876.

As far as Napier was concerned — even though the delta was some eighty kilometres away to the south-east — the bay for which he foresaw such a glorious future was 'the real mouth of the Indus'. Napier himself had demonstrated that a steamer could avoid the rough monsoon weather of the open sea by going via the salt creeks that lay between Karachi and the delta. It convinced him that once the port was developed '. . . the devil will drive trade like fire'. Before the end of the century he was to be proved right, but the development of the harbour which alone could achieve it was at first desperately slow.

Until 1852 merchantmen were unwilling to risk crossing the bar that lay at the bay's entrance. The royal navy's first survey reported it was of rock. That survey was then found to be wrong. The bar was of sand: still a hazard, but far less forbidding.

And inside the bay itself there were problems, notably the severe silting that took place whenever the river Lyari was in flood. The amount of mud left behind drastically affected the depth of water available to shipping. Reliable, year-round scouring of the basin was obviously needed; obvious enough, too, the means — to drive the sea tide itself against the mud build-up. How to make it happen, though, became cud for decades of disputatious chewing.

Finally, two massive structures were approved. First the Napier mole — a 182,000-tonne stone groyne built inside the harbour between 1861 and 1863. And then the stupendous Manora breakwater which still guards the sea entrance to the port. Completed in 1873, this 450-metre wall of 27.4-tonne stone blocks was erected in the sea on a foundation of rubble levelled off more than four metres beneath the low-water line. With other works these two great structures guaranteed a channel over the bar deep enough for the largest ships then afloat to cross in safety, and rendered the harbour safe from silting.

Above: Early morning bustle among a forest of masts at Karachi Harbour as the fishing fleet prepares to sail.

The consequences were evident immediately. By the turn of the century Karachi was the biggest wheat exporting port in the East.

That development continues. Perhaps most striking to the eye today are the mushrooming storage facilities on the oil jetty and the modern tanker berth capable of accommodating vessels up to 76,000 tonnes. But that's only one part of a building programme which by the 1980s had equipped the port with twenty-eight deepwater berths and saw it handling more than sixteen million tonnes of freight a year; a tonnage that is expected to double by the end of the century. And much greater expansion is envisaged after that: no fewer than 100 new berths to be completed by the year 2050.

And just as the mole named for Napier and the Manora breakwater underpinned all the port's subsequent development, so that development itself spawned the spectacular expansion of Karachi port's city.

By the end of the nineteenth century, growth was already considerable. Matching the lighthouses that had sprung up along the coast to assist the swelling numbers of ships using the harbour, the port railway lines, stock and sidings serving the wharves, the cranes, warehouses and administration offices inside, and the fine new Port Trust building and enlarged Customs House close by outside its gates, the town had started making durable marks on the thirteen square kilometres which it then occupied, with paved streets, courts, churches, government buildings, and commercial centres.

The grandeur of these structures speaks forcefully of the pride of their builders. Entering the inner yards of the Port Trust Building, for example, or climbing the steps of the later (1929) High Court Building, is to be reminded powerfully of that other age directly before independent Pakistan was formed. The experience is perhaps especially vivid in Karachi. Elsewhere in Pakistan — notably Lahore — the public buildings

Above: Jumbo prawns harvested from the wealth of Karachi's Arabian Sea waters will be deep-frozen for export to the gourmet houses of America, Europe, and the Far East.

of the British colonial period fuse into that improbable but highly successful style, neatly dubbed Victorian Mughal or Mughal Gothic. But Karachi shows little of that. The dominant characteristic of Karachi's greatest buildings is nineteenth-century British.

Nonetheless, without that alien, Victorian splendour, architecturally the great city would be impoverished indeed.

Guides to the town all give similar lists of the most important examples: the Masonic Hall built in 1845, for example, now headquarters of the Sind Wildlife Management Board; the Napier Barracks of 1847, now Government offices; the principal old churches (Holy Trinity, 1858, St Paul's, 1865, St Andrew's, 1868, and St Patrick's from mid-century); and — especially popular as a city amenity today — Frere Hall, opened in 1865 to honour Napier's successor as Sind Commissioner, Sir Bartle Frere.

Spacious gardens add grace and distinction to this landmark's somewhat stubby Victorian Gothic lines. And rightly, since the building was erected to honour one of the greater, more distinguished servants of the British crown in old India. Frere commanded the respect of his troops, initiated projects for the development of Sind, and — by cannily insisting that individual culprits be brought to justice, rather than adopting the then usual, arbitrary policy of punishing a whole tribe — even won the respect and admiration of law-breaking tribesman along the Sind borders. In recent years the hall has been renovated and decorated with paintings by the renowned Pakistani artist and specialist in Arabic calligraphy, Syed Sadequain.

A similarly prominent landmark in the old city is the Merewether Tower built to honour Sir William Merewether, third British Governor of Sind. It was Merewether who oversaw the building of the harbour's all-important Manora Breakwater. His monument, a clock tower erected in 1886-87, stands today at the hub of Karachi's downtown commercial area

amid the turmoil of traffic that sweeps incessantly by, seeming to strand it. So the monument tells not just the hour of the day but also of a tide in Karachi's history that long ago ran out.

Such structures and perhaps a dozen more — clubs, colleges, government, and commercial offices — are almost the only significant reminders of Karachi's early years. Almost.

There are, of course, the bazaars: not all equally old, but all worth visiting. They reflect the city's essential character as a centre of national and international trade.

The oldest ones grew by the harbour. Too narrow to accommodate pavements, crowded with tarpaulin-topped stalls selling dried fruit, textiles, grain, garlic, salt, spices, potatoes, sugar, copperware, pots, and second-hand clothing, their labyrinthine ways bustle with buyers — more congested, exciting, vivacious than the much bigger complex of bazaars, tourist shops, and modern shopping centres that make up Saddar, the biggest shopping area in the city.

In Saddar, each bazaar specialises in a single, different handicraft or line of goods. By contrast the countless little shops only too easily dubbed 'Aladdin's caves' sell the lot: onyx ware, copper goods, brass, hand-coated lacquer furnishings, wood carvings, handblocked printed cloth, Sindhi embroideries, jewellery — elaborately-handworked in silver or gold — ready-made or second-hand *shalwar-kameez*, cheap cotton shirts, luxurious fur coats, leather bags, women's dresses with traditional Sindhi mirror decoration, appliqué bedspreads, and handwoven carpets.

Pakistan is among the world's biggest exporters of carpets, and Karachi's bazaars sell them in every one of the country's astonishing range of styles and traditions, plus others from central Asia — Afghanistan, especially, and Kurdistan.

It's possible to grow weary in the jostle of a lively bazaar, but never

Above: Entrance facade of Frere Hall, one of Karachi's Victorian landmarks, built through public subscription and opened in 1865 to honour Sir Bartle Frere, Napier's successor as British proconsul to Sind. He was one of the British crown's most respected servants on the subcontinent.

Opposite top: Luscious fruits from the orchards of Pakistan's four provinces fill a Karachi market.

Opposite bottom: Gold and metal fillings gleaming in their containers, Karachi kerbside dentists patiently await their next customer.

bored. And besides, everywhere refreshment for the body is abundantly to hand — from the sellers of pure fruit juices who before your eyes press the succulent lemons, oranges, mangoes, pomegranates, sugarcane, or whatever else is in season that you fancy, to confections of all kinds of sweet and spicy cakes.

And also from the tea-counters that pour a truly sustaining beverage — sweet and thick because it's made with boiled milk (sometimes *in* the boiling milk); to the curbside vendors of hot, tandoor-baked breads — nan, paratha, chappati — and the whole mouth-watering variety of more substantial fare nowadays so favoured in western 'takeaways' but available everywhere in Pakistan's markets in dazzling abundance, tandooris, tikkas, kebabs, goshts, freshly-made halwa, and yoghurt besides.

The street stalls and counters by no means exhaust Karachi's eating out possibilities. Tikka houses abound, so do Chinese restaurants. There are drive-in snack bars — especially popular with the younger set — and in the biggest hotels many speciality continental foods. Karachi's top restaurants are noted for their excellent Pakistani cuisine.

All the liveliest reminders of Karachi's early days, of course, are near the harbour where the increase in trade first spilled into the town in an increasingly dense and chaotic *pot-pourri* of peoples, wares, and vehicles. Here the carts — donkey- or bullock-drawn — horse-drawn Victorias, camel wagons, even tram cars powered by steam locomotives, multiplied. It wasn't long before the locomotives were banned though, shortly before World War 1 broke out in 1914, for fatal accidents were becoming too frequent. Horses in Sola hats — to protect them from the hammer-heavy sun — replaced the steam engines until these, too, gave way to fuel power. The last tram was taken out of service in 1970.

Late twentieth-century traffic density is far worse than a century ago. The donkeys, horses, bullocks, and camels are all still there, still lugging their enormous wagon and cartloads stoically, unconcernedly, pitifully, or disdainfully, according to breed and size of load. The banished trams have been replaced by larger numbers of motor buses, mini-buses, taxis, vans, trucks and private cars, and also by many magnificently-ornamented trucks and lavishly-painted lorries which vie for space, bellowing for way, their amazing bulk in the confined space ever teased and tormented by the swarms of motor rickshaws that buzz, fizz, sputter, and jerk their way through, past, around (you almost expect *under*) them.

In, among, through and about this incredible twitching, panting, heaving, frustrated, vital mass of beasts and metal go the pedestrians — the vibrant young nonchalantly weaving for themselves a safe and sure passage, the cautious old carefully stitching theirs together. Combined, it's an awesome, loud, labouring, impossible — but gloriously dense and vivid — bedlam.

Karachi's phenomenal growth has made it one of the biggest cities in all Islam and its mosques and religious shrines befit its status. Of them all, the Defence Society Mosque is probably best known and most visited. Named from its location, it was built in the late 1960s and can accommodate 5,000 worshippers under its tent-like canopy. This fine dome, seventy-two metres in diameter, is the most striking aspect of the

Above: As his green parrot struts a line of sealed prophesies, a street fortune-teller anxiously awaits the moment when the bird of fate will pause at one envelope and thus unseal his client's destiny.

Above: Seventy-metre-high minaret complements the beauty of the tent-like dome of Karachi's Masjid-e-Tooba, the Defence Society Mosque, built without internal pillars and capable of holding 5,000 worshippers.

structure's unique, modern design, particularly inside, where its size is emphasised by the absence of pillars. Outside, a single, seventy-metre-high minaret complements the spread of the superbly simple roof.

The sea gave birth to Karachi, and the ever-mounting tonnage of goods it brings in and carries out, continues to nourish its seemingly endless growth. For many who know it — residents or travellers — the sea is also Karachi's principal attraction.

A bunder boat hired at Keamari, the Karachi Port, is all that's needed for one of the city's most popular outings — three or four hours spent catching crabs in the harbour. Such excursions are an institution and generally the boat crews, most of them residents of Babu and Bhit islands, inside the harbour, will have with them all that's needed for a meal to remember of boiled, or fried, fresh caught crab, complete with potatoes and onions, garnished with spices. They even have crabs on board with them, for passengers with unlucky lines.

Crabbing can be the delightful prelude to a rare and wonderful experience. Not far away is one of the few places in the world where, out of the deep, giant Green and Pacific turtles come to lay their eggs in the sands which, decades earlier, saw their own hatching. The beach, on the seaward side of the great bar of sand that protects Karachi's harbour, is one of two in the area; the other, Hawkes Bay, lies further west, about twenty-four kilometres from Karachi.

The instinct that guides the turtles back to Karachi's beaches remains one of nature's more tantalising mysteries. But its regularity can be observed, especially on moonlit nights between September and October. Singly, domed shells glistening, the mature females emerge from the wash of Arabian Sea breakers to drag their egg-laden bodies up the final stretch of their thousands-of-kilometres-long journey home. Above the high-water line they deposit their eggs deep in the sand.

Predators are legion. Apart from the pi-dogs and other animals that dig down to feast on the warm embryos, and the birds of all kinds that nab the pathetically vulnerable five centimetres of hatched mini-turtles before they can scuttle into the comparative safety of the (nonetheless perilous) sea — there is man. He has long hunted the turtle — celebrating nesting seasons with egg-taking and, for soup or the shell, capturing and killing the mature reptile.

In recent years, collaborating with the World Wildlife Fund, the Sind Wildlife Management Board and others have worked on a number of Marine Turtle Conservation Projects; but the extinction of these rare, endangered animals remains possible. The Sind authorities recognise a special responsibility: of nine known marine turtle nesting grounds in the world, they protect the only one which falls within the limits of a modern mega-city.

Outside that city's limits, in both directions, stretch kilometre upon kilometre of fine beaches. The more distant ones, wide, clean, filled with sun and innocent of crowds, offer bathing, surfing, scuba diving, and yachting, and except in the May to August monsoon season — when the currents are treacherous and caution is advised — all are counted excellent.

Near Gaddani, across the provincial border of Baluchistan, only forty-eight kilometres north-west of the metropolis, a new resort is growing in popularity among Karachi residents. Gaddani beach itself, however, has long been famous in a context that has nothing at all to do with leisure. There men break up ships; most of them virtually by hand. It is probably the biggest shipbreakers' yard in the world. The huge hulks — some of them 20,000 tonnes — are driven up onto the beach at high water and without ceremony, and amazingly little machinery, dismantled. You don't have to be a seafarer to find the great growing heaps of rusting metal, piling ever higher as the gaping sea-monsters come asunder, a strangely affecting sight.

Closer to Karachi the beaches are immensely popular as weekend — Thursday and Friday — playgrounds, especially at Clifton and on the sands of Sandspit, Hawkes Bay, and Paradise Point.

Of these, the wealthy suburb of Clifton is by far the most significant, boasting in addition to all the basic seaside amenities — refreshment stalls, tea shops, huts for day rent, souvenirs, and gaily-decorated horses and camels for rides on the sands — attractive gardens and a small amusement park, a well-stocked aquarium, and even a sea pier, built in 1923. The resort's greatest magnet, however, remains the Marine Drive, which every evening of the week unfailingly draws huge crowds of promenaders.

Clifton was favoured by the British. It was no more than a village on the seafront in the nineteenth century, but the Europeans appreciated the cool of its sea breezes a bare five kilometres from sweltering Keamari, and built some agreeable colonial-style houses there. Some are to be seen still, charming in their spacious, tree-shaded gardens.

In the twentieth century, the area has been the scene of much more substantial property development — commercial and industrial as well as residential — and most recently big money from outside the country has added walled residences of a flamboyance that clearly

Above: Snake charmer plays his flute as his defanged cobras sway on the sands of Hawkes Bay, a popular seaside resort twenty-five kilometres west of Karachi.

demonstrate their owner's wealth and their designer's taste.

Overall, however, most visitors will agree that today's Clifton looks what it has become: suburbia-on-sea.

Unless you look up to where, vivid on the hillside, a green and white striped dome attracts the eye. Decorated with flags and bunting it's an unmistakable landmark — and has been guiding Sindhi seamen home for more than 1,000 years. But this stripe-bright building is much more than a venerable aid to seamanship. It's the shrine of Abdullah Shah Ghazi, Karachi's patron saint.

'Baba Abdullah', as he is known, was a Muslim preacher. Apart from that, and his reputation for holiness and working wonders, little of certainty is known about him. But to the devout his memory is very dear and thousands visit his shrine daily — mendicants and musicians, scholars and simple faithful. A stream of freshwater flowing from a rock beneath his tomb is attributed to a miracle that he worked. In arid Sind, it could very well be so.

In Clifton, too, stands a Gothic red sandstone building, complete with dome and cupolas, known as Mohatta Palace. Sadly the house has been in decline since 1978 when its famous occupant, the Quaid's sister, Mohatarama Fatima, died. Conservationists have been campaigning for its preservation ever since.

Happily nothing of the kind is necessary at the birthplace of Mohamed Ali Jinnah himself. Secure in its own quiet dignity, at the junction of two streets in the busy old Karadar district, "Wazir Mansion" is preserved with a care that's tantamount to veneration. Appropriately so. The simple stairways, corridors and rooms, the casement exhibits of the Quaid's clothes, notebook, letters, cigarette case and house furnishings, the slightly fading photographs that convey so powerfully the austere pride of his legendary bearing, all encountered together in this old, hurlyburly quarter of a Karachi now twenty times the size it was when he named it the new-born country's first capital city, may well impress the thoughtful visitor with an almost religious awe at the amazing achievement of the child of this house.

Some measure of that achievement is to be found in Karachi's proudest monument — the mausoleum, or *mazaar*, of Mohamed Ali Jinnah. Like the man whose mortal remains it enshrines, the monument evokes many emotions; none stronger than admiration and wonder.

Erected on a hill just five kilometres from where he was born, the monument's grandeur pays its own eloquent and permanent tribute to the sheer scale of the triumph of a man who set himself determinedly against the floodtide of history and changed it; and in so doing altered the map of the world to gain for his people a land and government of their own.

But that grandeur in scale is dressed in the classic lines of extreme Mughal simplicity, effectively a white marble dome atop a matching, attenuated white marble cube. And whether blazing white in the dazzle of the midday sun or gently glowing under the concealed floodlights, the elegance of the clear-cut lines tells the secret of the achievement. For underlying all the Quaid's formidable armoury of intellectual strength it was, above all, his willpower and his single-minded dedication that won the triumph.

Following pages: Sundown over Manchar Lake, Sind Province.

You enter via lofty Moorish arches closed by handsome copper grilles. Inside, blue-glazed ceiling tiles from Japan provide the perfect foil for the spectacular crystal and gold chandelier above the tomb given by the people of China. A silver handrail from Iran, exquisitely proportioned, completes the monumental interior — surrounding, and setting apart, the last resting place of the man universally acknowledged as this country's Founder and Great Leader, Quaid-i-Azam.

Opposite: Sind farm workers bundle sun-dried hay.

The way the Quaid's city has expanded since his death excites a wide range of reactions from residents and visitors alike. Many consider it monstrous, for the overwhelming modernity which stifles its too rare relics of the past — where it doesn't tear them down — and cruel, for the harsh impact its stupendous growth has upon the living conditions of most of its inhabitants.

Other, by contrast, say it's like a salad bowl — with something for everybody — because of the number, the richness, and the variety of its cultures, and the unending train of newcomers that constantly strengthen and revitalize them.

Others again complain that Karachi is nothing but a megalopolis of migrants — with too many people in transit for enduring growth, and too many of the buildings that house them and the businesses that give them work here today, gone tomorrow. Karachi for these critics is nothing but a gigantic dormitory, 1,800 square kilometres big, jam-packed with victims of hardship, *en route* — they desperately hope and pray — from jobless penury to the bread they cannot earn anywhere else.

Exactly, admirers reply. Karachi lives — and gives life — and that's why Karachi thrives. Look at the city's economic importance to the nation; already in the 1980s it supplied almost a sixth of the country's entire gross domestic product. And it's still growing.

Indeed, observe moralists. And look where it's taking the city. The 'instant city' *par excellence* — the town of the moment, a would-be New York — where the poorest can hope to find instant work, instant gain, knowing that Karachi will also provide instant access to practically everything money can buy. But at what cost to the people, to the environment, and the country's traditional values?

None of the criticisms would suprise an urban sociologist. Karachi is very young, lacks discipline, and has grown too fast to take its own measure. Karachi, in fact, betrays many of the typical problems of youth: is callow, acquisitive, and does itself and its antecedents no favours. Karachi, the big city, has more than a slight tendency to lawlessness and — equally dangerous — to naive idealism.

The marvellous saving grace, of course, is its youth. This ever-expanding port city is undeniably gauche, brash, and unruly — but it is also exuberant, lively, energetic, and passionate. And its resourcefulness seems boundless. Probably only the old at heart really worry how the hectic, overgrown youngster will turn out. Certainly, to an outsider, nowhere else could symbolise the vitality of Pakistan better.

'Peccavi'
(Sir Charles Napier)

Karachi's location and commercial importance have made it the undisputed gateway to Pakistan. But huge and extravagant, young and without style, the brightly-lit sprawl tells the visitor practically nothing of the fabulously rich past of the land to which it gives access.

Happily, a journey outside Karachi quickly remedies that, and shows a crucial difference between the gateway and the country discovered beyond it. For whereas Karachi is founded on the sea, most of the rest of Pakistan's people, through literally thousands of years, have grown up by rivers — sometimes with life and death consequences for themselves and the communities they were born into.

Sind province — of which Karachi is the capital — lives by the greatest of Pakistan's many rivers, the Indus. The name of the province is in fact that of the river ('Indus' is simply the European rendering of the local word for 'river', Sindhu). To those who lived by it there is only one river: *the* river.

Originally of course the territory named from the river matched the river's extent — as far north as this was known — plus all the area of its influence east and west. Thus Sind originally included Kashmir, parts of Afghanistan, modern Baluchistan, Rajasthan and parts of Gujerat in India, as well as the territory it covers today. Unrealistically, but with sound logic, it has been remarked that since Partition in 1947 if any country is to be called 'India' it should be Pakistan, rather than its south-eastern neighbour; which, incidentally, in Hindi is called Bharat.

The supreme importance of the Indus to modern Sind is obvious from any map that shows population centres and transport systems. With the outstanding exception of Karachi — founded on the sea — and the roads to and from it, all else in the province follows where the river leads: whether to a city like Hyderabad or a major town like Sukkur or Larkana.

The rivers that pour down from the greatest concentration of mountain peaks on earth, making life possible in what would otherwise be an arid wasteland, run out onto an exceptionally flat plain. In the starkest possible contrast to the precipitous ravines and tumultuous narrow gorges that the rivers pour through earlier, this declines throughout its 1,600-kilometre length only fourteen centimetres to the kilometre. Only too easily the draining away of these tremendous waters across such a table turns haphazard.

Throughout the ages changes in the course of the Indus have entailed dire consequences for the cities of the plain and the galaxies of towns and villages around them. Indeed, the end of the Indus Valley civilization, centred on Moenjodaro and Harappa, is itself attributed by some experts to just such a diversion (the Indus today flows three kilometres east of its third millenium BC course beside ancient Moenjodaro).

Not infrequently through the centuries, riverside villagers and citizens have woken to find themselves waterless — or without the volume needed to grow their crops, deliver their goods, or maintain their civic or village status and economy. Dry and dustily insignificant little places on the other hand have suddenly and unexpectedly found themselves vital to trade and industry throughout a region. And consequently politically important. So, throughout Sind and lower Punjab it has always been the rivers that ultimately dictated the location and viability of communities.

Previous pages: Dominated by the ruined remnants of its still massive eighteenth-century fortress, the once-upon-a-time Sind capital of Hyderabad traces its ancestry back through more than 2,400 years of history.

Above: Ruins of a family mausoleum in the Chaukundi necropolis, on the outskirts of Karachi. This city of the dead is believed to date from the fifteenth-century but its origins are still unknown.

For this reason the abandoned, or greatly diminished, sites of yesterday's towns and villages often show where a river used to flow. Thatta is an obvious example.

Today three motor arteries cut their way through the desert surrounding Karachi. One drives north-west into sparsely populated Baluchistan. The other two both strike sharply eastward to cities on the Indus. The older of these two routes, known as the National Highway, presents a first, mysterious example of Sind history just twenty-seven kilometres out of Karachi.

The Chaukundi tombs lie low along the skyline north of the highway. From a distance — but for their golden sandstone glow — they could be taken for diminutive, relict, Greek temples. In fact they are nowhere near so old. They were probably built around the fifteenth and sixteenth centuries AD, and on closer inspection the rectangular blocks of finely-incised stone, laid in narrow, pyramid ascent on similarly carved, larger blocks, wear more of an eastern than a western look. Typical individual tombs are between sixty and ninety centimetres wide at the base, between 1.5 and 2.4 metres long and anywhere between 1.2 and 4.2 metres high. Some, more elaborate, are grouped in families and surrounded by a protective quadrangle or circle of pillars surmounted by beams. Some of these 'families' of tombs are roofed over.

Apart from the shape of the tombs — 'chaukundi' means 'four-cornered' — their main feature is the extraordinarily-rich carving all over them, intricate and delicate as work in wood. Similar designs, in fact, are used by woodcarvers today, and on Sindhi and Baluchi textiles, pottery, and jewellery. Men are depicted in stylized turbans, occasionally riding horses. There are warriors and weapons. The women wear jewellery.

Similar cemeteries have been found in a number of places along the Makran coast in Baluchistan and up the Indus as far as Sehwan Sharif;

but none outside Sind and Baluchistan. The stone at Chaukundi was quarried at Jungshahi, not far from Thatta, seventy-two kilometres further east. Virtually nothing else is known about the tombs, and nothing at all about the people who built them. But the place seems to have been used for burials from time immemorial.

Under a clear blue sky, amid bougainvillea and birdsong on a high desert plain otherwise relieved only occasionally by acacia bushes or trees, the Chaukundi tombs are a pleasing sight. They rest the mind. And their quiet, after the hurlyburly of Karachi, seems deepened by the traffic that races past almost as if in another world — more seen than heard — less than a kilometre away.

About thirty-two kilometres further down the National Highway a road sign points the way to Banbhore — believed by many scholars to be where Mohamed bin Qasim landed, bringing Islam to the subcontinent, in AD 712. If they are right, the place has a remarkable distinction, for it must then be considered the seedbed of today's Pakistan — which was formed precisely to provide a subcontinental homeland for the millions who now live by the teachings the young general introduced nearly thirteen centuries ago.

Certainly, at that time a large town stood on this spot, and for nine centuries before that smaller settlements. The large town lasted into the thirteenth century when it was abandoned. The fortified citadel area and the lakeside residential area collapsed — to be quickly smothered by sand and become the huge mound which scientists have only this century probed.

What confronts the parties of excited young schoolchildren being shown round, the serious students, the family groups enjoying a weekend outing together and the many casual visitors from overseas is a large, low-lying dugout area where, typically in Pakistan — even on the most renowned sites — one is free to roam, and pick up fragments of pottery from the past and dream of the people who made and sold and used the bowl or cup or jar it was once part of in that ancient seaside city and wonder what became of them and what occasioned their city's end.

Because this is a mystery. Banbhore — or Daibul as it was then called if this is where bin Qasim landed — was clearly a well-planned, well-defended and prosperous port city, with large public buildings, and widespread residential areas with stone-built, lime-plastered homes for the wealthy and stone foundations for even the poorest mud brick dwellings. The ancient harbour, now half-submerged, yielded pottery and coins that point to strong links with both Muslim countries to the west and China in the far north-east. Clearly this was an important trading centre: possibly the Karachi of its day.

Skeletons with arrows among their bones, found in the ruins of homes reduced to ashes, suggest that the port may have been sacked — perhaps by the Afghan warrior Jalalludin. Was that what caused the definitive collapse of the once proud port city in the thirtenth century? Impossible to say yet. Perhaps the next cubic metre of sand an expert painstakingly sifts will give the decisive clue . . . .

The main reason why some believe this is the ancient Hindu port of Daibul is clearly visible — the floor and the foundations, both intact, of a mosque. It bears the Islamic date 109 AH (AD 727). This is therefore the site

Opposite: Possibly the first herald of the nation that would be born 1,250 years later, this mosque at Mansura, near Hyderabad, symbolises the enduring faith which created Pakistan.

Opposite: Light and shade enhance the vaulting of Shah Jahan's classic mosque at Thatta.

Above: Intricate mosaic of delicate pastels testifies to the superb restoration of Shah Jahan's mosque, Thatta.

of one of the oldest mosques in Pakistan — possibly the oldest.

Why, at the head of 12,000 troops, the seventeen-year-old son-in-law of Hajjaj Bin Yousuf, the Governor of Iraq, was sent into Sind is also unclear. One Arab account says it was to punish the Sindhis for attacks on peaceful Arab merchants. Another claims that it was ordered because of the pillaging of one of the Caliph's ships returning to Bagdhad with gifts from Sri Lanka. Whatever inspired it the young general achieved dramatic success. After taking the Indus delta towns he pressed his attack up the Indus to Multan, and in a campaign of only a few weeks made all that territory, including the stronghold of Multan, his.

Some seventy per cent of Sindhis quickly adopted the way of the Prophet. Sind therefore counts its conversion to Islam from this time — earlier than the rest of the country. It's estimated that today perhaps two per cent of Sindhis remain Hindu in continuity with their pre-bin Qasim forbears.

It's been suggested that Banbhore is the port Alexander the Great founded in 325 BC, before he sent his fleet off to rendezvous with him further west down the coast on his ill-fated way home. It's highly

imprprobable. Undoubtedly the conqueror of the fabulously powerful
Persian Empire came this way on his return to Babylon; or at least his
admiral Nearchus did. But because of the amount of silt the Indus
deposits daily — said to be of the order of one million tonnes — it's
estimated that today's shoreline is eighty kilometres further south than it
was in Alexander's day. A stronger contender for the honour — though
apparently still unlikely — is Thatta.

Nowadays eighty kilometres from the sea and rightly described as a
dusty little village, Thatta was at one time an important port — the
capital, no less, of lower Sind. Its story exemplifies perfectly the
insecurity that has always attended the towns and cities the inconstant
Indus makes great.

From the fourteenth to the nineteenth centuries Thatta flourished,
taking in its prosperous stride both sacking by the Portuguese and siege
by the dethroned Mughal emperor Humayun. But in the middle of the
eighteenth century the Indus took its life-giving waters some distance
away to the east, and Thatta's resulting decline was accelerated by the
arrival of cheap textile imports from Britain which undercut what had
been a staple local industry. When its capital status too was taken away
and moved further up the Indus — at first to Khudabad, but soon
afterwards to the Kalhora stronghold of Hyderabad — Thatta's
regionally significant days were over.

For all that, the dusty little village possesses a gem that will always
bring pilgrims. Dating from the days of glory, Thatta has one of the
Mughals' most glorious mosques.

Begun in 1647 by the architect Emperor Shah Jahan — builder, for his
wife, of the Taj Mahal — and all but completed by the last of the great
Mughal monarchs, Shah Jahan's son Aurangzeb, the mosque now stands
as splendid and dazzling as ever, at the edge of Thatta's shrivelled past.

*Above: Midmorning light warms one of the many
thousands of mausolea, tombs, and graves that cover
the fifteen-square-kilometre necropolis of Makli Hill,
near Thatta. Most of the structures, dating from
between the fourteenth and fifteenth centuries, were
built on classic Mughal lines for kings, queens,
poets, saints, generals, and scholars.*

Above: Five hooded badgirs *on the modern Aga Khan Maternity Hospital, Hyderabad, maintain a centuries-old tradition of air conditioning. Built facing the prevailing wind, the* badgirs *trap whatever breeze blows during Sind's torrid summer and channel it to the rooms below.*

It is a triumph of restoration, because this jewel had fallen into serious disrepair and had to be extensively renovated by the government.

Today it is easy to sense the original splendour of Thatta's mosque — memorable for blue glazed tiles, wonderfully delicate mosaics, and the innumerable domes that cover it. Different guides quote widely differing numbers of these, but all agree in attributing the mosque's remarkable acoustics to them. Prayers recited at the *mirhab* can be heard throughout the building.

The hot climate explains a feature of the buildings in this part of Sind, known as a *badgir*. This is a wind scoop — a cone capping the roofs of many of the buildings — made of wood, mud, or cement. They are open on one side to trap whatever cooling breeze blows, and channel it to the rooms below thus airing the houses. In appearance *badgirs* are remarkably like the hoods used on the oasthouses of Kent, in England, and like them are an established feature of architectural design. Even modern builings like Hyderabad's new Aga Khan hospital have used it — to pleasing effect.

The blue glazed tiles so coolly dazzling at the mosque are another feature of this region, and with mosaics and domes they characterise the many monuments in Thatta's other great tourist haunt, Makli, or Little Makkah — one of the most remarkable of all cities of the dead. It's a favourite tourist stop.

Situated on the Karachi side of old Thatta, the six square kilometres of the Makli Hill cemetery are said to contain no fewer than one million graves, tombs, and mausolea. They make an impressive — if somewhat chilling — celebration of the dead. Many of the tomb structures were obviously originally of breathtaking richness, but sadly in some cases the years have taken toll even of the monuments built to preserve the memory of those who were great yesterday.

Most of the tombs date from the sixteenth and seventeenth centuries, though some go back as far as the fourteenth. Kings and queens, military leaders, governors and saints, philosophers, poets and famous scholars are buried here. Scale, and the quality and quantity of ornament, vary considerably, but the stone engravings are generally considered masterpieces — so regular one could imagine them stamped on the stone, as at Chaukundi, not carved.

Recent tombs from the Arghun and Mughal periods wear the beautifully glazed and enamelled tiles and bricks that are still typical products of the area. There is much to admire. And yet . . . .

Maybe it's the very grandeur of some of the monuments that makes the mind philosophical; or perhaps it's the contrast between dead splendour and the livewire vivacity of hand-in-hand kiddies going into the shrines with their families, the beauty of the lovely, laughing girls in their multi-coloured, elegant dresses, the tourists snapping the squatting charmers of beady-eyed cobras near the gate, and the poor lads earning only abuse for insisting on cleaning a just-cleaned car outside. Makli indeed holds much to admire, but there's no forgetting it's a necropolis — a vast sun-filled camp of the dead.

For loud, squawking life go to Kheenjar Lake — only a few kilometres to the north of Thatta. This part of Sind is on many bird migration routes and Kheenjar is one of several lakes that provide welcome winter R and R facilities for weary ducks, geese, heron, flamingos, pelicans, egrets, cormorants, and kingfishers escaping northern gloom. Two smaller lakes were joined to make Kheenjar a 300-square-kilometre reservoir for Karachi, but it serves also as a game reserve popular with picnickers and visitors using the overnight bungalows. Haleji — an attractive but smaller reserve closer to Karachi — has similar amenities.

And then, beyond Kheenjar, visibly aged but only the more strikingly vigorous and energetic for that, is Pakistan's third largest urban centre, Hyderabad. Certainly pre-Islamic in foundation, it's among the oldest living cities on the subcontinent. This is where the modern Super Highway — third of the three main roads out of Karachi — ends. *En route* it has passed the approach to Kirthar National Park — a protected refuge for the almost extinct Sind wild goat and the urial, the striped hyena, leopard, and other rare wildlife.

The Super Highway is hardly the most attractive of Pakistan's main roads, but it provides a fast — if at times hair-raising — four-hour sprint through the desert that separates Karachi from its ages old senior city. And since desert accounts for much of Pakistan's surface area this can be a valuable first look at that sometimes seemingly endless, tawny challenge to eye, throat and mind.

Deserts vary. Few conform to the commonplace image of a flat — or endlessly evenly undulating — waste of sand without vegetation. Scrub accompanies the Super Highway on both sides practically all the way. The first kilometres out of the seaside city are quite flat but suddenly there are hills, and with them long, and low, flat mounds. Nearer the road the unbroken chain of power pylons ties the desert scenario in with Pakistan's urban industrial upgrading programmes; while telegraph lines — following the snaking of the tracks that carry Pakistan Railways' green and yellow carriages the length and breadth of the country — relay the deals done by businessmen, the anxieties of families, the secrets of lovers, unsuspected, across the arid plains.

On the edge of Hyderabad city all traffic converges at a level crossing. Bulbous buses crammed to the rooftop with passengers and their bursting bags and baggage, overloaded trucks sporting legends of prosaic wisdom and despairing love ('If you have money come to Lahore; if you have nothing stay away' — 'I love you but you don't want me'), reckless vans and battered cars, diminutive road-weary donkeys with precarious loads and staring drivers, spunky motor scooters, bikes bristling with mirrors, friendly inquisitive pedestrians ('Where are you from? How do you like Pakistan? What are you doing in Hyderabad?') and the growing group of the curious attracts the gypsies peddling bangles and tangerines, wristwatches, Seven-up and wrapped sweets till slowly-smoothly the passengers in the train are passing through our staring-up midst, staring down at us from a metal box world as if *we* were the strange ones . . . .

Hyderabad was capital of Sind until the British Governor Napier transferred the honour to the fledgling Karachi; but already by then Hyderabad had long been very long in the tooth. Hereabouts, centuries before there was a Roman Empire — let alone a British one — Alexander the Great rested his homesick troops. Ten and a half centuries after that the much younger warrior, Mohamed bin Qasim, fighting his way north

Above: Dating from 1914, this clock tower built during the British occupation overlooks one of the city's bazaars and is one of the more recent additions to Hyderabad's hybrid architecture.

to Multan, captured the town here — then called Neroon. And that happened half a century before Charlemagne.

The busy city of Hyderabad seen today was laid out by the Kalhoras — a dynasty which claimed to have come over from what is now Iraq with the conqueror Qasim. They decided to develop Hyderabad in the 1760s when the fickle Indus changed course and abandoned Khudabad — which only a few years before, also courtesy of the Indus, had displaced Thatta as Sind capital. But twenty years later the Kalhoras themselves yielded control of the region to another local family, the Baluchi Talpurs, who ruled for the next fifty-five years.

It was outside Hyderabad, at Miani in 1843, that the British led by Napier and the forces of the Talpur Amirs fought the decisive battle for control of Sind. The outcome enabled the English general to put his classical education and skill as a punster to some practical use. He sent London a single Latin word cable: 'Peccavi' (I have sinned).

The fort Napier won — structurally much reduced but on its four square kilometres of high ground still today a massive presence brooding over the city — was built in 1768 by Ghulam Shah Kalhora. Today its most impressive feature is the forty- to fifty-foot-high defensive wall, with merlons shaped to resemble, at night, the shadowy figures of soldiers on guard.

The Mirs Haram, or seraglio, is a single room about nine metres square with a wooden verandah, a door and windows on each of its four sides. It preserves enough wall painting and lacquer work in the ceiling to give an idea of the once remarkable beauty of the interior. The west door also shows finely worked, original wood carvings.

The room overlooks the colourful Shahi bazaar, Hyderabad's main shopping area. This winds its way from outside the fort gates through 2.5 kilometres of dense-packed alleys making and selling Sindhi embroidery, hand-painted prints, silver and gold jewellery, the typically pointed shoes of the area, perfumes and bangles, until it reaches the clock tower that straddles the main way with all the assurance of age; although in this venerable city it's a chick of a building — erected only this century, in 1914.

Hyderabad's principal monuments are shrines. In the heart of the city the devout come in large numbers to kiss a stone slab believed to be imprinted with the outlines of the hand and foot of the fourth Caliph of Islam, Hazrat Ali. Nearby is the shrine of Hazrat Abdul Wahab Jilani, a member of a famous Baghdad family related to the Prophet.

The monumental Kalhora and Talpur tombs are generally massive late Mughal constructions. One — that of Mian Ghulam Shah Kalhora (1756-72) — is protected by an enormous mud wall that encircles it like a prison, although once inside this impression is dispelled immediately.

The octagonal mausoleum rises from a marble floor and is surrounded by a balustrade of carved yellow sandstone. It is embellished with lovely, blue-glazed bricks and lacquered tiles. At floor level the interior walls are decorated with a low marble frieze carved with floral patterns. Tiled panels, frescos, and inlay cover the wall above and elaborate intaglio in the arches completes the graceful effect of marble pilasters. The tomb itself is of marble, and carved with delicate, floral patterns, like the frieze.

The overall impression is of great wealth and grandeur — and waste.

Opposite: Spiked gates of Hyderabad's 225-year-old fort, built in an era of warring dynastic factions.

Above: Carved window balcony — one of the few surviving testaments to Hyderabad's former splendour as a civic and cultural centre.

Pigeons, crows, sparrows, swifts, and foreigners seem to be the only ones who care.

Hyderabad has a good, small, modern museum, the Sind Provincial. The four galleries cover Sind pre-history, archaeological — from Buddhist to British — ethnological and industrial (artefacts), with attractive displays informatively set out. The city's university, situated nearby at Jamshoro, enjoys a first-class reputation. Its Institute of Sindology boasts a fine collection of manuscripts and coins.

There are several lakes around Hyderabad and permits can be obtained for winter hunting of grey partridge, duck, wild boar, and hog deer. It's a popular tourist attraction.

One hundred and sixty kilometres east of Hyderabad stands a Rajput fort settlement known as Umarkot — or Umar's Fort. It's a very pleasant road, tree-shaded and cool most of the way, and the single tarmacadam track prompts many a thought about the beauty of this world and how attached to it you have become and how much you wish drivers — your own and those of oncoming vehicles — would not insist on seeing the whites of each other's eyes before giving way.

Happily there is plenty of unmade road space each side of the track, though even then your car can still be swept by cattle fodder overhanging a lorry, truck, or cart loaded — it seems to be a rule — to a minimum of twice the height and three times the width of the vehicle carrying it. In other words the drive to Umarkot is not uneventful — you do not sleep — and well worth undertaking, not just for itself and the good of your soul, but especially for the history that waits at the end of the road.

The ruler Umar was the first of the local Sumrah family which, starting with him in 1050, ruled Sind for three centuries. From the crumbling but largely intact walls of his half-a-square-kilometre of fortress, with its semi-circular bastions guarding the four corners and main gate — and yet more easily from the nineteenth-century central tower — extensive views of the surrounding Thar desert show the isolation of fort and township. To north and east is the arid Rajasthan zone of India; to the south the Rann of Kutch.

In 1541 Humayun, son of Babur, the founder of the Mughal dynasty, was driven into this inhospitable terrain by the Afghan Sher Shah Suri. And nearby, on 23 November the year after, his young wife, Hamida Begum, gave birth to Akbar, whose very name — meaning the Great One — foretold the eminence the child would reach in the history of the subcontinent.

By the time of Akbar's birth the hapless Humayun was down to seven horsemen and a handful of followers, and though unexpectedly welcomed by the Rajahs of Umarkot had failed in his bid to evict the Afghan ruler of Sind.

Yet he foresaw his babe's destiny. Distributing musk to celebrate the birth of an heir he predicted, 'The fame of this new-born baby will one day fill the earth like the fragrance of this musk'. *Ben trovato* or not, the words fairly describe the renown Akbar achieved during his crowded life and his half-century upon the Peacock Throne.

A gratifyingly solid but low-key monument, of four low and simple stone arches, united by a shallow dome, celebrates the birthplace. One

face of the structure bears an inscription in Sindhi with an English translation. Beneath the monument an older stone carries the record in Sindhi. Grander monuments proclaim the achievements of the grown man — notably in the ancient walls of Lahore, and most importantly in the stability he gave to a Hindustan of many diverse peoples, faiths, and cultures. But there is something agreeable about the modesty of Umarkot's tribute to the place where he was born — in a region which, with all the rest of Sind and Baluchistan, he was to restore to Mughal rule long before his death in 1605.

Even while he lived portraits showed him with a halo, and it is a fact that it was Akbar who bequeathed to his successors the 'divine' authority which attached to the Peacock Throne — if not to all its occupants — till the coming of the British Raj in the nineteenth century.

Umarkot fort has a small but attractive museum with displays of weaponry from Afghanistan, beautifully scripted Persian letters written

by Akbar's most trusted courtier, Abdul Fazal, collections of Mughal poetry, histories, scientific treatises, miniature paintings, legal documents from the reign of Akbar, and specimens of Farsi and Urdu calligraphy.

In all but its modesty it reflects the richness and range of Mughal civilization.

Forty-eight kilometres northeast of Hyderabad — just off the National Highway — the prosperous little township of Bhit Shah guards one of Pakistan's most attractive religious shrines and, quite independently, hosts a colony of Government-sponsored artists and artisans.

The Sindhi word 'Bhit' means sand dune and refers to the only feature the area could boast in the late seventeenth century, when the now much revered Sufi mystic Shah Abdul Latif arrived. He found the loneliness and desolation perfect for his contemplative way of life and pitched his tent. He lived all the rest of his days there and was buried where he had lived.

The contemplative was also a poet. His output centred on two profound but simple ideas which have found new favour amid the turmoil of a very different century — the twentieth. It is that all creation is one and that love embraces every human being.

At any time of the year, but above all on his feasts, the shrine courtyard attracts large crowds of pilgrims — notably folksingers, accompanied by the ancient Sindhi *alghoza* and two-stringed *dotara*, who recite the verses of this Poet of Love. Dervishes dance in ecstasy, and in the emotion-charged atmosphere of the celebrations it's not unusual to see the music, lyrics, dancing, and drums move people to tears.

The shrine, which is quite superb, is reached by way of marble-floored courtyards and archways where young girls squat, weaving garlands of red roses.

Under a domed and minareted roof the arched facade of the holy

Above: Smiling Hindu woman and child, one of Pakistan's few minority communities.

Opposite: Guests celebrate a Bhit Shah wedding at a shrine built to honour the saint, Shah Abdul Latif Bhati.

Top: Hala artist hand painting ceramic tiles before glazing.

Above: Dates and coconuts on sale from a Bhit Shah street vendor.

man's mausoleum is coolly distinguished in the dominant blues of its glazed tiles; white floral designs with green detail — buds and blooms — providing relief. Inside the portico the mirror work so popular in the ornamentation of the great buildings of Pakistan's plains is much in evidence — green and red-painted in more floral designs, like those carved into the marble about the door. The ceiling, supported on carved marble pillars is of carved wooden beams and tiles in alternating combinations of blue-green-white and brown-yellow-green. An elaborate screen encloses the tombs of Shah Abdul Latif and his cousin Jamal Shah.

Adjacent to the mausoleum is a mosque — its exterior face likewise in blue and white. Inside there is much mirror-work around the walls of the three bays. Floral frescos by local people cover the ceiling as background to inscriptions from the Qur'an.

The glazed tiles which are such a feature of the Bhit Shah shrine, as of all important buildings throughout Sind and the Punjab, are a traditional product of Hala — a small town three kilometres north of Bhit Shah. Hala has always enjoyed an envied reputation as a handicrafts centre — woodwork, pottery and lacquering among others. These are all still practised in the narrow streets behind the prettily decorated mosque, but between 1975 and 1981 a Government-inspired co-operative scheme was fostered in Bhit Shah, and many of Hala's craftsmen moved with their families to help set up what has become an artisans' colony. Known today as the Sind Small Industries Corporation they aim particularly at the export market, where their products — all quality goods — sell well.

As always in the presence of master craftsmen — but especially when novelty adds to the mystique — awe seems the only possible response to the spectacle of men bent, literally, to the task of lacquering the sticks, poles, legs and posts that will make vivid and multi-coloured beds, armchairs, tables — and nowadays garden swings.

In the cool of a verandah the workmen sit on their low stools with an arrangement of pegs and wooden and metal bars fixed in the ground before them. The gear is meaningless — until the artisan settles to his work: fixing the wood to be lacquered between spikes, revolving it with a steady bow-string sawing of his right arm, all the time using his feet up and down a metal bar to control the staining he applies with the colour sticks in his left hand.

Most impressive to watch is the incalculably deft use of tools to remove a later stain (or stains) to reveal — in astonishingly regular geometric patterns — colour or colours applied before; the right arm maintaining the hypnotically regular sawing motion that drives the wood being stained round and round. It's like watching a man's feet and hands magicking gorgeously bright, wax-shiney colours onto a once-bare wooden bobbin.

It takes five years to learn this glamorous tip of the industry's tree. Others select the wood — of different kinds — and bring it to Bhit Shah where it's carved to order in the homes of the artisans before being brought for lacquering. The lac too is locally prepared — mixed with colours and processed in the homes.

Altogether there are seventy-five families of craftsmen in the Bhit Shah colony — among them specialists in ajrak textiles, handloomed cloths, pottery, printing seals and glazed tiles. These are all traditional Sindhi handicrafts — in the case of the glazed tiles and the ajrak work thousands of years old; the others at least centuries-old.

The ajrak process is complex beyond words: starting, forty days before it will finish, with 100 per cent locally-made Pakistani cotton which is boiled, dried, soaked in vegetable oil and dried again. A first colour change is made by soaking in a chemical bath, and this is rendered maroon by painting on a mixture of glue, chalk and water. The wooden tile stamps are cut on the spot to intricate, traditional designs which are applied by hand to produce the particular pattern wanted. Bobhar — buffalo dung — is used to dry it.

Next the patterned cloth is colour-dipped for one minute in a ground tank, then sun-dried, washed in a canal, and soaked and boiled in another colour for two hours, and so on. It's then washed again, and again sun-dried. Different patterns are used for the fringes.

Ajrak colouring takes two years to learn and is practised in many other places besides Bhit Shah. It makes the rich dark patterning completely colour fast. 'Boil it!' the men boast. 'The colours will live longer than you . . . .'

Or would you like some handloomed silk? Mohamed, taught by his father, and now teaching his own son, will climb into the loom he built in the window of his shop and, if you wait one hour, produce a metre before your eyes. The process — marrying warp and weft — offers an apt image for a scheme that provides a twentieth-century industrial and marketing framework for the preservation and development of centuries-old skills.

In many ways it's like Pakistan itself: an interweave of ancient traditions, crafts and cultures with twentieth-century technology and economics — like the mega-dams of Tarbela and Mangla that harness the power of rivers still crossed downstream by bridges of boats; like the nomadic tribesmen who still drive their sheep up dry river beds as they have done through the ages, but now in a country where the main hospitals practise nuclear medicine and radiotherapy; like the camels, donkeys, and inflated cowskin rafts that share the burden of transportation in this ever-ancient, ever-new country with articulated trucks, jet-powered aircraft, and 76,000-tonne oil tankers plying in and out of Karachi's ever-expanding harbour.

Hala stands halfway between the sea and the great barrage the British erected on the Indus at Sukkur in 1932, and is one of the places downriver that monitor the river's floodwaters. One major effect of the Sukkur barrage and the other brakes subsequently placed on the river has been to reduce its meandering. But this makes the river no more predictable, and not much safer than it was before. Even in recent years, shifts in course have exceeded two kilometres. Because of the quantity of water carried in the flood season, monitoring is absolutely essential.

The river's unpredictability may have something to do with the relative absence of historical sites along much of the eastern shore between Hala and the approaches to Sukkur. Whatever the cause it's quite different on the opposite bank. There you come face to face with reaches of history now recognised to be as significant for mankind's history as any yet found on the surface of earth.

But first a diversion for castle-lovers. About thirty kilometres north of

Above: Using a twentieth-century soda bottle, a passer-by taps the bole of an ancient Neem tree, a reliable source of liquid refreshment in drought and heat, at Umarkot only a few metres from the spot where Akbar the Great was born.

Hala, on the western shore, a track leads off westwards for some eighteen kilometres to Ranikot — a castle erected by Talpur Amirs in the nineteenth century. With no less than twenty-four kilometres of circumference walls it seems likely that the claim that the fortress is the largest in the world is right.

The vast enclosure — which accommodates two separate forts — may occupy the site of a much earlier fortress that guarded the important trade route between the old seaport of Thatta and the cities of central Asia. Remains of Arab caravanserais have been found along the way.

But Ranikot is literally by the way. Barely seventeen kilometres further north, on the river side, a much less impressive but far more important site is just visible from the highway.

The eight hectares of excavations at Amri appear to be no more than another extended mound of earth a kilometre from the road. They will leave the layman none the wiser for stopping to take a look — unless he or she uses imagination. For the work done here has told archaeologists of people who lived *before* the great Indus Valley centres of Moenjodaro and Harappa were founded about 2,500 BC. You stand, in fact, in one of the first places on earth where the human animal attempted civilization: at about the same time as others, 3,200 kilometres away to the west, were making a similar experiment on the banks of the river Nile.

A comparison with what those ancient Egyptians achieved is instructive. Every child knows of the pyramids, the most obvious of the many great epitaphs they left. Less obvious is the fact that the Egyptian design for city living reflected their absolute dependence on the flooding of the river. The yearly phenomenon bred an awe, a fatalism, and a subservience to the pharaohs that was tantamount to slavery. Thus while the pharaohs' palaces and life-style accorded with the fabulous scale of their tombs, nothing remains to show that the mass of Egyptian people — whose labour in the fields gave life to that marvellous 'Old Kingdom' — counted for anything at all except as a work force.

In striking contrast the Indus Valley civilization built no pyramids like Egypt, and no ziggurats like Babylon. Its people in fact seem to have built nothing at all higher than fifty feet. Their artefacts, too, compare poorly with Egypt's and Mesopotamia's. What they did produce, however, was if anything more astounding; for they built cities that can only be compared with the kind of modern, middle-class city suburb being built today, more than 4,000 years later. The physical order — the planning that went into the making of Moenjodaro — is staggering; but nothing, compared with the consideration for all citizens which it shows.

Here at Amri that eventual sophistication was broached. Archaeologists have identified the foundations of flat, rectangular houses of various sizes, with doors and mud floors. Some had mud-brick walls. Pottery too was found — thin, well-made, cream or pink in colour, with decoration in black — and beads and terracotta animals. There was an early overlay of the later Moenjodaro standard of development. Then nothing. What happened — whether the entire settlement shifted north to share in the great social experiment of Moenjodaro itself — is not known. But on the meaningless-looking mound of Amri — as at contemporary sites in the other provinces of modern Pakistan — you stand where began what the pioneering archaeologist Sir Mortimer

Opposite: Elegant mosaics adorn the entrance to the tomb of Lal Shahbaz Qalander, the twelfth-century Dervish scholar who is patron saint of Sind.

Above: Mausoleum of Sind poet and mystic, Abul Wahal Faruqi.

Overleaf: Breathtaking facade of Abul Wahal Faruqi's mausoleum exploits the ceramic tilework for which this region on the Sind-Punjab border has long been famous.

Wheeler called 'a story of human enterprise and understanding such as has occurred only a few times in the history and prehistory of mankind'.

Moenjodaro's own legacy is still more than 160 kilometres to the north. Before reaching it the road goes through Sehwan Sharif — the town with probably the longest history of continuous occupation in all Sind.

The ancient town, built on a hill not far from the Indus, may have attracted Alexander the Great to found the fort whose ruins stand in impressive command of both town and river. Coins dating from his era were found here. From here too the brother of Chandragupta II ruled a Buddhist kingdom; and from Mohamed bin Qasim's eighth-century conquest onwards, Sehwan has never been absent from history's pages — dominating as it did the trade route between upper and lower Sind.

What brings most visitors to Sehwan today, however, is not trade but the shrine of Hazrat Lal Shahbaz Qalandar. The last part of the name is important — a title approved by scholars for only three saints in all the history of Islam. It refers to the belief that the Qalandar's life was ordained directly by God.

Lal Shahbaz — the name means Red Falcon — was a Persian born in Azerbaijan in 1177. He lived to a very great age, dying at Sehwan in 1274. He was a dervish sufi, missionary, scholar and poet, a noted grammarian and religious leader, and he wrote books in both Farsi and Arabic.

Every year from all over the country his feast attracts devotees — Hindu as well as Muslim — and the dervishes in their long robes, beads, bracelets and coloured headbands whirl, entranced, faster and faster to the mounting excitement of pulsing drums, gongs, bells, cymbals, and horns. The setting is fine — the mausoleum, like that of Shah Abdul Latif in Bhit Shah, once again faced with predominantly blue-glazed tiles that make a cool and dignified backdrop for the feverish excitement and heady religious fervour.

Opposite: Lake Manchar boatman using traditional bow-drill for repair work on his fishing vessel.

Above: Like a dream in yellow, a young woman drifts by an island on the waters of Lake Manchar.

West of Sehwan is Manchar Lake — an immense, natural, shallow depression of marshes and Indus overspill. Like the other lakes in Sind it attracts huge colonies of birds and is well stocked with fish. It's a beautiful body of water — especially when, beyond the sharp green of the banks of reeds shushing against one another in a fresh evening breeze, the sun glistens on the shimmering waters before ballooning crimson and slowly sinking behind the distant hills.

What's especially interesting about Lake Manchar is its boat people. They live in a floating town of high flat-bottomed boats. Some are Mohanas: a minority tribe of fishermen who spend all their lives afloat in this part of the Indus valley. They live by fishing, catching wildfowl in flood seasons, and ferrying people and goods to and from the small villages of the local rural communities. They fish with net and line but use a more picturesque method to hunt waterfowl — wading out chin-deep with stuffed birds as cover for themselves and their old firearms. (It is in fact remarkably easy to come close to the nests of waterfowl old enough to be left by their hunting parents but still too young to fly away).

What makes the Mohanas especially interesting is the number of points of contact between them and the ancient civilization of Moenjodaro — including their distinctive boats (similar to the ones depicted on the famous Moenjodaro seals) and the fact that they hold their traditional annual festival at a point on this enormous river opposite Moenjodaro. The site, of course, was not known until 1922.

Independently of such circumstantial evidence, linguists quarrel with the claim that Moenjodaro means the 'Mound of the Dead'. People would never call the city they lived in by such a name, they say. A more plausible meaning, they suggest, is 'Mound of the Mohanas'.

Back on the main road from Manchar Lake the way to Moenjodaro runs north via Khudabad — briefly capital of Sind before it was Hyderabad's turn, but nowadays just a small town surrounded by mosques and old tombs — and then Dadu. From here the road stays in close touch with the railway most of the eighty kilometres to the marvellously preserved, but now threatened, remains of one of the two chief cities of Indus Valley civilization.

Moenjodaro is a tough challenge to the imagination that tries to put it in historical context. Julius Caesar is half a millennium closer to us than he is to those who built this place. Alexander the Great stands midway between us and them. While Egyptian rulers were dragooning a servile people to build pyramids to honour dead pharaohs their contemporaries here thought out and created man's first drawing-board city.

The mind struggles to assess it. If Moenjodaro had stood alone, and lasted fifty years, it would surely be counted some kind of fluke: fantastic, quite inexplicable, and without rival anywhere in history; but still a fluke.

Moenjodaro, however, was far from being short-lived and anything but alone. There's a twin, Harappa, 560 kilometres upriver — discovered first and tragically, as we shall see — and there are more than seventy other known sites which are integral to this civic empire.

Time-lapse photography at this point in the Indus Valley 4,500 years ago would have shown a vast plain — the creation of a formidable river

and fertile along its shores — intermittent marshes carrying jungle and wildlife, scattered settlements of struggling farmers, an occasional camp of nomads . . . . And suddenly a city . . . .

The suddenness is a fact to come back to, but first the city.

It's enormous in extent — more than five kilometres round — and laid out meticulously on a grid system. Roads run north-south, east-west. Generally the main roads are on the north-south axis, with link roads east-west. Building regulations are strictly adhered to, and the greatest care taken to prevent any structure from encroaching upon the streets. In some districts the houses are bigger and better built; in others, noticeably smaller. But all show obvious concern for the well-being of the occupants and meet basic standards of construction and amenities.

Thus, all are brick-built, and nearly all have at least two stories, with brick stairways to the higher floors. The houses, generally, are built around a square-, or slightly oblong-shaped courtyard: open to the sky and surrounded by rooms. Entrance is normally from a side street — presumably because the main roads are busy during daytime.

Inside there's a vestibule with passages that lead to the kitchen, pantry and living rooms. Most of these have windows high above floor level. They're covered by alabaster lattice because the summer sun is scorching hot.

Each house has its own well in the courtyard or, where this is lacking, easy access to a public well in a nearby square or piazzetta. All wells in the city, incidentally, are bricklined: and revetted at the top so that children and domestic animals can't fall in.

Each house has its own drainage system — bricklined conduits leading to main drains that run down the middle of the street below pavement level. Apart from periodic inspection holes these drains are everywhere securely covered with flat stones and sturdy tiles. Elaborate grading ensures that the waste is deposited outside the inhabited areas.

Many houses have garbage chutes too. The rubbish empties into external pits that are cleared by official garbage disposal workers. There are small reserved areas on some streets — apparently for city workers or gendarmes to keep equipment; or shelter from the sun or rain.

Away from the mathematically precise layout of the houses, streets, and city districts the marsh and river waters that might have been expected to imperil such an amazingly contrived city have been channelled to safety in nearby fields. Possibly this also serves an irrigation purpose: although the climate here in 2500 BC is wetter and the valley naturally more fertile. But the city has been built right next to the river, so a 1.6-kilometre-long embankment has been constructed, to protect it from periodic flooding.

Elsewhere, on the city's edge, there's a large quarry, with a nearby brick kiln. It generates a busy traffic in jungle timber to fuel it. The roads are full of traffic — pedestrians and uniformly-designed carts drawn by pairs of bullocks — hauling felled trees or bringing fodder for the animals and vegetables, wheat, barley, and cotton to the city's commercial and residential districts, and up to the citadel area that dominates the scene. Here there are enormous public buildings, a huge granary and, the centrepiece, what can only be a ceremonial pool.

Perhaps the busiest area of all is the waterfront. Trade is a central activity of the empire with grain, cotton, pottery (identical to that made locally today) going out and many perishables coming in — together with alabaster, bitumen and steatite, silver and lead, tin, turquoise and lapis lazuli, copper, and semi-precious stones. Moenjodaro's women are obviously very fond of jewellery: they wear hairpins and earrings and strings of precious and semi-precious metals and stones. They seem to like their skirts short and their hair high.

The steatite brought in from Baluchistan is used for identifications of different kinds: mainly for traders' seals stamped on goods passing through customs or taxation formalities, but also as hallmarks for business houses and even as amulets or as individual identity cards. Of all the artefacts left by the Indus Valley civilization these are universally admired.

Steatite is a soft stone, easily carved, and the artistic talent of these little-known people appears here at its best. The small seals — generally only two to four centimetres square — carry superb animal engravings (domestic, jungle, mythical) and a so far undeciphered script (presumably giving the trader's or bearer's name).

Many boats ply the river; some to go downriver to the sea and the start of a 3,200-kilometre-round trip north-westwards along the Makran coast to settlements that share their own culture, as far as modern Bahrein.

That's already beyond the westward extent of their 1.2-million-square-kilometre empire — Egypt's was 37,000 — but it doesn't satisfy the pioneers of Moenjodaro. They travel overland too to trade with Mesopotamia — where cotton comes to be called 'sindu' (and in Greece 'sindon') — as well as to northern Afghanistan, and north-east to the Ganges basin and south-east to communities beyond the Rann of Kutch.

They are conducting what Sir Mortimer Wheeler was to call 'the vastest experiment in civilization before the Roman Empire'.

And just as its physical spread was much greater than Mesopotamia's and Egypt's combined, so its civilization was more pervasive. Neither of those others was civil the way Moenjodaro was. Even in ruins the city shows a sense of civic responsibility — of concern for the collective welfare of the whole community — that is entirely absent from the others. In this it's much closer to modern society than either of its contemporaries.

There was a vastness too, in the stride that lifted them so rapidly to that peak of social organisation. Archaeological evidence shows relatively little experimenting. At Ur in Mesopotamia it shows a high street that lengthens as it wanders — obviously not knowing how far it will go, or which direction it will face when it gets there. Moenjodaro could not be more different. Its builders knew exactly where they were going and, moreover, the style they and their descendants intended to travel in.

Whoever they were — and it's assumed they came originally from the great Irano-Afghan massif — they seem to have got their incredible experiment in vast urban living right, practically from the beginning. Settlements in places like Amri to the south, Kot Diji across the river and, most interesting, Harappa itself doubtless gave these fantastic innovators something to base their ideas on.

But without detracting from what was done by way of preliminary, none of it can begin to compare with Moenjodaro or Harappa or the empire that together they seem to have headed. For the sites excavated reveal a staggering uniformity — even at the limits of the vast area the empire covered; one that extended over several centuries not only in house design and drainage, town planning, and apparent economic unity, but right down to the size of bricks used, the shopkeepers' weights, the housewife's pots and pans, the design of carts and boats, jewellery, and children's toys. And most improbable of all: this vast empire, so far as is known, was held together by consensus.

What amazing social maturity these people possessed! If we wonder who invented the wheel — what he, or she, was like? — similar questions must be asked about those who pioneered the making of Moenjodaro. Who found the way? And having found it by what magic did they persuade contemporaries to try it, and make it work?

Work it certainly did: for most of 1,000 years. And here was no servility of the kind that piled pyramids at Gizeh. The citizens of Moenjodaro clearly approved the formula: at least twice Indus floods forced them to rebuild wide areas of their city. They did. To the same standards they'd enjoyed previously.

What kind of authority could organise early society so? The script that may contain the answer has yet to be deciphered, so speculation centres on the citadel complex and the figure now generally referred to as 'the priest-king'.

It makes sense. The citadel, raised to the west and looking down on the city, would have caught the first and last light of the sun — and so have been the first and last reality borne in on the minds of the town's inhabitants. Next to it was the huge granary, and the bafflingly elaborate eighty-square-metre pool, two metres deep in the middle, which no one who sees it in its surroundings and with all its adjuncts can surely believe was merely a secular washtub. The suggestion that it must have been of ceremonial, and probably religious, significance would seem right.

In a society so deeply involved with natural forces like the river, floodings and drought, over which they had no control, it seems likely that some kind of animism would have been central to the State outlook. In fact, some have attributed much of the development of Hinduism to the Indus Valley civilization.

In such a scenario it would be natural for whoever was 'high priest' of the ceremonial conducted at the citadel pool to have also been the supreme arbiter of order in this most orderly of societies. Thus the notion of the 'priest-king' is now taken almost for granted in connection with Indus Valley civilization. Karachi museum shows an Indus Valley statuette usually described as the priest-king. Unquestionably he has the qualities of distance and austerity which seem to go with a primitive religion.

If, indeed, such a figure was the pivot of that characteristic Indus Valley order it could help to explain the moral force of the Indus Valley idea: rather as the great Mughals after Akbar benefitted from the righteousness he bequeathed to Mughal rule. Disobedience in such societies is worse than criminal; it is blasphemous. Conformity is virtue and, in the root sense of that word, strength. That strength, in the

Indus Valley empire, kept a civilization flourishing.

The end of Moenjodaro and all the cities and towns that subscribed to its ordered ways seems to have been as sudden as its origin. Excavators say that at the end building standards fell way short of what went before. The sparkle was gone. The society was in decline. There were catastrophic floods, quite distinct from the annual snowmelt. And there is strong evidence that water that had already passed downstream flooded back (perhaps from earthquake?) and may literally have drowned Moenjodaro.

There's also evidence of some violence — dead bodies left uncovered — which was not the Moenjodaro way. Perhaps the Aryans who invaded the lowlands about this time hold the answer.

Or perhaps it was a combination of some or all these factors. Whatever the cause, it seems that throughout its range this amazing civic empire ended more or less abruptly: not to be matched until Roman force of arms imposed the *Pax Romana* from Hadrian's Wall in the north of Britain to the Caspian Sea, and from the Danube to the Sahara.

For anyone seriously interested in Pakistan, a visit to Moenjodaro is essential. But it may well be that the deepest impression will not be made by the precise layout of the city or the meticulous care evident in the design of the houses, or the almost obsessive preoccupation with drainage — or by the exquisite beauty of the ancient steatite seals, or the mesmeric gaze of the 'priest-king' statuette. Not, in fact, by any of the features of that astonishing civilization, in themselves.

Instead, the greatest impact will almost certainly be in the seen continuities. The design of the carts encountered on the roads and the boats on the river and nearby lakes around Moenjodaro today is practically the same as those in the steatite seals made 4,500 years ago. Similarly the shards unearthed and made whole again in the museum display cases are identical to the pots thrown on the wheels and sold in the shops of nearby Larkhana.

And since the people who built this phenomenal civilization here had already domesticated all the animals now used in Pakistan today you can look at the boys watering the dour buffalo in the roadside canals and marshes — shouting, prodding with sticks, crying out with teeth-bright laughter — and know you are looking here at the authentic rural profile of this country in an image that goes all the way back to the most extensive and most triumphantly civil of all the known ancient civilizations.

Ironically, the Indus which gave this incomparable achievement life — and which may have drowned it 800 years later — has been helped in recent years to menace its excavated remains. Ten years after they were uncovered irrigation schemes of such magnitude were inaugurated upriver that the water table at Moenjodaro rose more than six metres (in 1980 it was fluctuating between 1.5 metres in October and 3.6 metres in May every year).

The result was that structural remains which had been preserved underground like a bee in amber through forty centuries began to disintegrate. In 1964 one expert warned that if nothing was done the site would be lost before the end of the century. Much has been done; but the scale of remedy needed defies international, not just national effort. The

Above: Sindhi schoolboy, in traditional hat, intent on learning.

war to save the site is being waged on three fronts: groundwater control, protection against Indus flooding, and conservation of the structural remains. Sadly, victory is far from assured.

There's a happier story immediately opposite Moenjodaro, however, on the other side of the Indus where, crowning a steep cliff, one of the best-preserved castles in the country overlooks the highway. No need to strain the imagination to appreciate this superb Talpur fort — built early in the nineteenth century during the reign of Mirsohrab Khan (1787-1847).

The merlon-topped fortifications are its most striking external feature. Inside — apart from the castle's immense size — it must be the three gates that bar progress up the steep, winding roadway. Dangerous with huge, naked iron daggers on mounts the size of shields, the mere sight of these gates pierces the mind. Medieval Europe's fortified gates and portcullises by comparison are puny.

There was reason in these massively cruel beds of spikes, of course. They were to stop elephants used as battering rams — not men.

Inconceivable as it may seem when you stand before them that an enemy might penetrate such fiendish obstacles, the fort is said to have a tradition that only the first two gates should be contested; that an invader who took them should be accounted victor and admitted through the third. Certainly you will feel that anyone who can fight his way through two of these deserves to win.

Yet Kot Diji's greatest claim to fame is as the site of the Indus Valley's earliest-known fortress: parts of whose ancient walls the visitor to the Talpur Fort passes through.

This ancient Kot Diji is older than Amri, and almost certainly one of the places the builders of the great civilization whose capital stood across the river learned from. There was a citadel area for the elite and a separate artisan zone — the other side of the road from the Talpur fort — where houses were built of mud and stone. Good pottery was made, with colourful, painted designs. The women wore necklaces, garlands and bangles, and the children played with toys of stone and baked clay like those found at Moenjodaro; but made two or three centuries earlier.

And then nearby is one of those places that jerks the strings of the mind away from both the origins of civilization and our nineteenth-century yesterday and illustrates the length, breadth, and depth of Sind history by drawing attention to a selection of dates in between.

Nothing much remains of the ancient city variously named Aror and Alor, but interesting things are told of it. Alexander the Great's whole army is supposed to have stayed there and fortified the place. It was capital at the time of what was considered the richest province in all India.

Almost 1,000 years later the Chinese Buddhist pilgrim Hsuan Tsang came for a visit: and wrote that Sind stretched from Kashmir to the sea and was ruled by a Buddhist king — a state of affairs, however, that did not last much longer. First Hindus seized power and then in AD 712 Mohamed bin Qasim arrived and in another of his lightning strikes on the way to Multan vanquished the Hindus and assumed control.

Least credible, but easily the most colourful of all the stories is the

*Above: Royal pavilion in the foreground, the
battlements of the nineteenth-century Talpur Fort at
Kot Diji stretch far into the distance.*

one about how the Indus changed its course — to more or less its present
bed west of Aror.

One day in the tenth century a merchant grew so angry with the harsh
trading conditions the local ruler wanted to impose on him — among
them that the merchant should present the ruler with a favourite slave
girl — that he decided revenge was the only adequate response.

Asking for three days to think about the prince's terms he went off —
not to meditate but to hire men to dig a new channel for the river, away
from the ruler's city, blocking off the old channel with the excavated
earth. On day four the ruler and his people are said to have woken up to
no river. Improbable as this story may be, in ancient times, certainly, the
river has flowed both east and west of its present line, and still floods
over both banks.

In fact, the Indus at Sukkur — less than eleven kilometres west of Aror
— does not meander at will through the plain but cuts through a narrow
limestone gorge. This was a major consideration in the choice of Sukkur
for the first — and in the view of many still one of the most impressive
— barrages on the river Indus. It was proposed in the 1840s at the same
time that Napier was trying to get Karachi's port development under
way, but nothing was done to implement the idea for most of a century.

The plaque commemorating its inauguration on 24 October, 1923, by
the Governor of Bombay, Sir George Lloyd — whose name the barrage
bears 'at the request of the people of Sind' — explains that, with its seven
allied canals, it was designed to irrigate 3.2 million hectares of land in the
province of Sind and the state of Khairpur (a small Talpur state, still then
independent).

It was, in fact, the major undertaking in the creation of what was then
the world's biggest irrigation scheme. Within eight years wheat yields
had increased fivefold and cotton threefold. Sadly, however, irrigation

raised the water table to levels that have caused serious salination — and loss of productive land.

The problem is constantly encountered in Punjab, but already in Sind the hoar-frost-in-summer look of salinity blights too many fields. It's seen along the road from Sukkur to Jacobabad, beside which the numerous pools of floodwater also attract, more agreeably, large flocks of birds — especially during the winter migrations. This part of Sind is a rice-growing area and the correction of salinity — by the use of perforated underground pipes — is a government priority. Development of the district's hydroelectric and natural gas resources is also under way.

Jacobabad is only a handful of kilometres from the Sind-Baluchistan border and Baluchi influence is strong. In fact, despite the modernisation of the economy, socially the region is heavily tribal with regard to both land ownership and community organisation. It still bears something of the 'frontier' quality that was its outstanding characteristic when General John Jacob — for whom it is now named — arrived in 1847. Jacob's mandate was to pacify tribesmen technically subject to the Baluchi Khan of Kalat but in practice showing allegiance to no one.

The Englishman adopted a clear and positive policy of pursuing and bringing to justice the individual lawbreaker, instead of imposing sanctions on their tribes, as was the common practice before. In this way, and by demonstrating respect for the Khan's area of jurisdiction, Jacob won respect for himself.

He also developed the township which now bears his name — building roads and houses, planting trees, and digging canals. A prodigious worker, a great administrator and gifted innovator he also found time to invent the first working two-bore rifle and to design and build a beautiful wooden-cased, chain-driven clock. It's kept, still in immaculate condition, in the house where he lived and died — nowadays the District Commissioner's residence. The clock tells the time on two faces and shows the phase of the moon, the month of the year, the date, and the day of the week. The handle that winds the movement looks big enough to start a bus.

In the cemetery a monument beside the large table of marble that covers his tomb remembers Jacob as a 'distinguished soldier and administrator'. It's the perfect tribute. Jacob died, aged only forty-six, in 1858.

Above: Camel dance at a wedding reception.

3 Garden in the Wilderness

'Our bed the thorny bush
The ground our pillow.'
(Baluchi song)

The green fields on the edge of Jacobabad give place within a few kilometres to a sandpaper flat, stone-strewn wasteland. You are in the Kacchi desert of Baluchistan — Pakistan's westernmost, largest, least-populated province.

One and a half times the size of the United Kingdom, but with only one-thirteenth its population (4.3 million compared with 56.4) the province is an area of immense potential — almost all of it yet to be realised. Of all unexpected strengths the one which is most developed is agriculture. Baluchistan contrives to be the Garden of Pakistan.

Emptiness soon surrounds you — waste, as far as the eye can see, forwards, backwards, to left, to right. And the further you go from Jacobabad the more you feel it all round you — at you. The awareness can be exhilarating. It can be disturbing.

In fact, some relief from the emptiness stalks the way: just over a kilometre west of the road, running parallel to it, is a line of power pylons, and on the other side of the road, idle under the sun, the track of the Sukkur to Quetta railway line. Both pylons and railway are in regular use, but because of the desert backdrop the pylons always, and the track most of the time, wear the look — like the road — of enterprise abandoned. Still, even in their silence they show that humankind has been here before you. Without them you could doubt it.

Indeed, if any place on earth deserves to be called a desolation this is it — act one scene one of creation: a flat desert floor before the reject materials, the ragged rocks and stones, have been tidied away ready for scene two, when the lake, river or sea is to appear and bring on the shrubs, trees, life. Nothing lives here yet. You're on your own.

Or so it seems. Far off to the east a brief, thin, easily-missed line of trees can now be made out, suggesting water. So it does exist — out there, near the horizon. It only emphasises the otherwise unrelieved aridity of the endless, featureless, sun-blasted panorama.

The scenery is typical of Baluchistan. The province was painted on the grand scale, with enormous, uncompromising sweeps of the brush, and only two features suited the immensity: mountains and deserts. True, the southern limits of this province account for most of Pakistan's 800 kilometres of coastline. But it's the desert wastes, like the Kacchi, and mountains — interspersed with high plateaux and arid hill basins — that define Baluchistan's character. The mountains, in particular, determined its shape.

The province is roughly like two squares of land. One is huge — with the Arabian Sea on the south, Iran to the west, and Afghanistan along the northern edge; the other, two-thirds the size, overlaps the larger square's north-eastern corner. Quetta, the provincial capital and the only significant urbanised region, in the smaller square, overlooks the Afghanistan border, just north of where the squares join.

The road from Jacobabad enters the province, and the Kacchi desert, halfway across the base of the smaller square. Further east, down the side of this square, are the southern reaches of the Sulaiman Mountains. Nearly 500 kilometres long, north to south, they mark Baluchistan's north-eastern flank. With their dramatic scarps, plateaux, steep, craggy outcrops, terraced slopes, and alluvial basins they present

Opposite: Young Baluchi herdboy poses in smiling celebration of spring in the rocky grandeur of the Bolan Pass as he leads his stock to summer pasture.

Previous pages: In the harsh light and heat of a cloudless day a camel train moves along the dry bed of the Bolan River to reach summer pastures before the first floods.

a quite extraordinary landscape. In the Takhte Sulaiman peak they reach a height of 11,295 feet.

Down the eastern side of the larger square, south-west of Jacobabad, is the much lower Kirthar Range. Its highest point — Kutte Ji Kabar, or Dog's Grave — is 6,878 feet. Here the valleys are cultivated and the hills support flocks of sheep and goats. But this range, too, is bleak, rugged and — above 4,000 feet — barren.

Across the top of the smaller square, down its western side through Quetta and continuing into the larger square, run more mountains — those of the mighty Toba Kakar Range. They enjoy a unique distinction. They alone of Baluchistan's mountain ranges are clad with trees — juniper, tamarisk, and pistachio.

South of Quetta, fanning out westwards like the fingers of a giant hand across most of the large square, from the Afghanistan border in the north down to the Makran coast in the south, is a series of other mountain ranges, all naked and barren.

Besides framing the province, these mountains are Baluchistan's natural fortifications. That's how they're seen by the people, who sing of their peaks as 'better than an army', of 'the lofty heights our comrades', and of 'the pathless gorges our friends'.

This 'natural army' has a splendour all its own. Jagged and eroded, the ranges show the most amazing strata — folded and twisted with the violence of the earth movements that made them — and bizarre rock formations. They are also quite improbably colourful: striated with greys, greens, reds, black, turquoise and purple, and so betray the presence of many minerals.

In the high, barren plateaux between these ranks of peaks, oases are rare but where they occur they're surrounded by fields and orchards in strikingly colourful contrast to the sunbaked waste.

Still, it's mainly unforgiving country.

Whether there are oases or not, the Baluchi people don't seem much worried. 'Our drink is from the flowing springs' they boast; 'our bed the thorny bush; the ground we make our pillow.' They are indeed hardy people. They have to be to survive in such an environment, for besides bare mountains and deserts there's little else apart from two enormous salt pans — the larger of them, Hamun-i-Mashkhel, eighty-six kilometres long and thirty-five kilometres across — in the north and north-west. After rains there are numerous waterways, vital but short-lived.

Like all hardy races the Baluchis have great pride. 'The beauty of the night is in the stars; and the beauty of the forest is in the Baluchis', so they say of themselves. In truth, they are people of high pedigree, descended from the Chaldees who founded ancient Babylon. Cyrus, creator of the Persian Empire, banished them when he conquered Babylon in 539 BC so they became wanderers living in various inhospitable regions from Kurdistan to — eventually — Baluchistan.

There are many Pathans in Baluchistan, too. In fact in the north-west of the province they form the majority. The Dravidian-speaking Brahuis are fewer in number but have special claim to attention. Many ethnologists believe they are from the same stock as the pioneers of the Indus Valley civilization. They would have gone down from the high plateaux of Baluchistan through the Sulaiman mountains into the much more fertile

Opposite: Shallow depressions in the baked earth of what was once a fertile wetland are the earliest-known evidence of domestication of cattle. They are among the countless relics of 5,000 years of continuous settlement between the eighth and third millenniums BC at Mehr Gahr, south of the Bolan Pass. The depressions are thought to be the foundations of cattle stalls.

alluvial plain created by the Indus River system.

Doubtless because of the ruggedness of their way of life, the qualities Baluchis prize above all others are the eminently virile, public ones: strength, courage, status in the tribe, personal honour, the keeping of vows, friendship, and hospitality. Traditionally they live by breeding livestock — especially sheep — from which they take milk, cheese, meat, fuel (from the dung), and rugs, coats and bags (from the skins).

Settlement in this rugged land, away from the urban areas (mainly Quetta) which account for about one quarter of the province's 4.3 million people, is inevitably sparse. Population density is said to be about twelve souls to each square kilometre, but the figure is hardly to be taken seriously, since more than forty per cent of the province's families are nomadic, or semi-nomadic.

In this unpredictable environment, the mobility of livestock makes them an important factor in the provincial economy. But the pastoralist life-style is far from easy, as extracts from a gazetteer published in the first quarter of this century — and still relevant — show:

January/February: flocks shelter from the cold, rain, snow, in huts and caves. Fodder — dried grass and shrubs collected the previous spring . . .

Above left: Baluchi tea vendor offers sustaining cup of sweet, milky tea to refresh the thirsty traveller.

Above: Mini-Macey's in a remote region of Baluchistan offers a range of everything from beads and silk scarves to beans, nuts, and cigarettes. Such deceptively small cabin-stores carry a surprisingly wide range of goods.

March: grass and shrubs start to shoot. Fodder still fed. Lambing.

April: weaning of kids and lambs to quarter milk. Risk of west winds damaging pasture.

May: grass abundant, cut and stored. Shearing. Making of *shi* (clarified butter) begins. (Continues till July).

June: grass starts to dry. Milk yield falls. Male goats and rams sold off.

July: weaning and castration of wethers. Ewes go dry. Browsing on stubble.

August/September: grass now dry; some green on the shrubs. Sheep shorn; rams join sheep in some areas. Flocks down to the plains from Quetta;

October: rams loose; sheep fattened for killing. Flocks subsisting on dried grass, leaves, shrubs.

November/December: fat sheep killed for *landhi*. Grazing very poor.

Bleak as the grazing pattern reads — with barely one month of fresh grass and little shrub greenery — it's still more than this harsh land can sustain nowadays. Overgrazing has led to the loss of edible species in many areas and their replacement by poisonous and inedible ground cover. The reason is less in the land's inability to recover than in man's failure to use its resources with the necessary understanding and social discipline. It's a classic case of what's today called "desertification", much easier to identify than to remedy.

At Independence in 1947 all the tribal areas acceded to Pakistan. At that time Baluchistan was considered the most backward area in the entire subcontinent, possessed of a grand total of five industrial units: two fruit preservation plants, an ice factory, a flour mill, and a chemical-pharmaceutical plant.

Attempts to develop the province have increased through the years — with textile and wool mills at Lasbela, Bolan, and Harnai, and a variety of factories in the capital, Quetta, and elsewhere. But the inevitable shortage of infrastructure in such a vast, and relatively unpeopled province means progress is slow and the traditional tribal independence of spirit does not give way easily.

Central to any possibility of change are the *sardars*, the traditional rulers (tribal chiefs) of Baluchistan. During their period of rule the British confirmed the sardars' powers and privileges while retaining overall regional control. But historically these tribal rulers have shown more concern about maintaining their own authority over the people than with social and economic progress. They are said to be tyrannical, believing that might is right, and nomadism favours their rigidly hierarchical control. But their power makes their attitude crucial to future development.

Written literature, also considered essential nowadays for development programmes, is a modern attainment, although Baluchistan boasts several centuries of oral tradition — all of it, however, preoccupied with prowess in battle. Concern for the language has come with Independence. Until 1962, when the Baluchi Academy was founded to encourage it, the language did not enjoy official patronage — whether under Afghan rule, Persian, Hindustani, the Brahui Khan of Kalat, or even the Talpur Baluchis. All of these used Farsi as their court language.

Gradually, nevertheless, changes in the ancient Baluchistan way of life are beginning to take place. The great seasonal migrations, for example, from summer grazing in the mountain plains down to the warmer lowland pastures in winter and then back again in spring, were organised in large colourful caravans, strikingly picturesque against the thick, gravel, Pleistocene-age river beds they travelled along.

Nowadays the same water courses are followed but you no longer see the great caravans of the past; only small family groups with a donkey or two, oxen, oxcarts loaded with the family possessions, and a camel effortlessly transporting several women and young children, a clutch of young chicks, and a kid or pair of bleating lambkins standing unhappy but somehow perseveringly on the great swaying back — as well, of course, as all the pots, pans, and general baggage swinging and clatter-clanging about the animal's flanks.

It's still normal for these semi-nomads of Baluchistan to travel 300 kilometres or more like this, but their own economy is changing. It depends less and less upon the raising of stock and more and more on jobs in trade and transport, on handicrafts, and even on settled farming.

None of this drama of social change and economic development is visible as you drive north from Jacobabad along the metal road towards Sibi and the provincial capital, Quetta. By now three or four bulging buses may have passed — going the other way, to Jacobabad — and a handful of overloaded trucks.

Otherwise in the ninety minute, almost eerily lonely drive, the only relief from the bleak, stony-sandy flatness has been a party of horsemen galloping briefly beside the silent railway track (where did they come from?). In their multi-coloured costumes they look like some Mexican cinema setpiece. (Did they dynamite the rails? Are they on their way to rob a bank?) Half an hour later, on the other side of the road, a string of camels trot contemptuously off to camp by a mirage of tree-edged seashore on the north-west horizon. Famous country for mirages, this. On the horizon you can see, in the sea that isn't there, the upside-down reflection of the trees that aren't there either.

Otherwise the road just goes on — with only you and the pylons, the railway lines, the slate-grey surface in front, and the desert either side. All the world, it seems, is desert . . . and illusion . . . until just before Sibi, 160 kilometres north-west of Jacobabad, where crops again grow and, well back from the road, the occasional home or shop appears.

You probably don't realise it but you have just travelled — in winter temperatures around 35° C — a region that becomes so hot in summer that only the southern Sahara, north-western Australia, and one other place in Baluchistan — the Turbat Valley in Makran — compare. Jacobabad has recorded 53° C. Sibi's June average exceeds 45° C. (A Persian poet, addressing God, asked why Hell had to be created when there was Sibi . . . .)

Hardly to be wondered at that the scorching wind in that season is said to kill man and beast. In such conditions, whatever work must be done is completed in dawn hours. By midday life is at bay and people lie indoors in the best dark they can make — not re-emerging until late in the afternoon. Hills like the Brahui about Quetta give relief to those lucky enough to be there then; though they exact winter tribute, of sub-zero temperatures with or without snow.

Above: Baluchi youngster in traditional headdress.

Above: Young Baluchi scholar absorbed in his study of Qur'anic scripture.

This Sibi has a deal of history attaching to it. Mahmud of Ghazni, successfully campaigning to bring Punjab, Sind, and Baluchistan into the Afghan Ghaznavid Empire, occupied it in 1005. Five hundred years later, Ameer Chakar Rind, champion of Baluchi unity, defeated the Sindhi Sammah rulers in battle there and built a mud fort which still stands. The British occupied the town too, for a short time in 1841 and later used it as a rendezvous for negotiations with tribesmen, when they were trying to set up a *'cordon sanitaire'* around Sind.

Today Sibi is surprisingly, and pleasingly, spread out, with broad avenues and frequent trees. Its annual horse and cattle fair, which dates back to 1496, attracts tribesmen from all over the province still. But the town proper stands a little way off the main road, and if there are no lights — as can happen if there is no electricity ('load-sharing' it's called in a wonderful example of 'bureaucratese'; really of course it means 'lack-sharing' . . . .) — it's possible to miss the turning.

And now, down the road beyond Sibi but before Quetta, wait two more of those special treats for tourists which other countries can sometimes match but never provide, as Pakistan seems to, round practically every other bend in the road.

The first is the archaeological site of Mehr Gahr — a neolithic settlement that shows Baluchistan played a dominant role — and not just a 'bit part', as was thought earlier — in the development of urban civilization in the subcontinent. The other, the Bolan Pass, is to many people more spectacular than the now much better-known Khyber.

Investigation of the extensive Mehr Gahr find — roughly sixteen kilometres west of the Sibi road at the foot of the Bolan Pass — is in the hands of the French archaeological team which discovered it in 1984. The various excavations are on flat sandy levels in the middle of a vast and rugged, pebble-bedded basin. To date, evidence shows that the site was continuously occupied for five thousand years — from the eighth to the third millenniums BC — before, therefore, the Indus Valley civilization of Moenjodaro and Harappa. More than that, evidence from the early, hunting period shows the presence of twelve different species of large animal, some now extinct.

Mehr Gahr is the first neolithic site in the world that shows people gradually changing from the use of wild animals for food and clothing, to the use of domestic — sheep, goats, but above all cattle. It gives the first evidence of hump-backed breeds. It shows that barley and wheat were cultivated and, from 5,000 BC, cotton. Crafts practised here included the use of lapis lazuli and seashells for ornaments, and later the production and decoration of pottery, and representation of people and animals.

Ivory was used, and copper. So were seals. There is also important evidence — the seashells, for example — of long-distance trade exchanges with Iran, the Makran coast, Central Asia, Afghanistan, and the Indian Ocean. Graves show that the dead were buried in the flex position, and children separately from adults.

Anyone happy enough to find the site will be astonished at the quantity of sherds and flints that have been amassed, and excited by whatever other evidence of such long-ago, organised human habitation he can identify.

Above: Baluchi women fetching water from a tube well.

But the deepest satisfaction is likely to be in the realisation that in this very place, watched by these very same mountains, under just such skies, a mere 10,000 years ago the air rang with the shouts, cries, and laughter of men and women — and their children — who were the true pioneers of the way we live today.

These great pioneers were among the first to learn how to grow barley and wheat and how to store what they produced; the first to learn to domesticate and raise sheep, goats and cattle, and husband them on a scale that would keep them and their children alive; among the first to broach the crafts of pottery, metalwork, tool-making, and jewellery that made civilization not just possible but agreeable too, and desirable.

No surprise that experts see in the Mehr Gahr village settlements the seed of the fantastic Indus Valley city that was to blossom later.

Back on the main road it's only a few kilometres to the Bolan Pass. Historically, and still, this is one of the most important ways through the mountains that hedge the subcontinent from the rest of Asia.

A feature of the mainly sun-filled Bolan Pass is the abrupt way the river cut through the higher reaches of the mountain stone. Progress

Above: Chickens safely aboard with the pots and pans, a young Baluchi girl drives her family's heavily laden donkey to new pastures.

northwards along, up, down, and around its snaking ninety-five-kilometre passage is marked by the steady disappearance of the transitional slope between the flanks of the mountains and the bed of the river, shared in the dry season by pale blue pebbles, thick gravel deposits, streams, and surprisingly large stands of palm and other trees.

At first, the sand-coloured cliffs lean back in sphynx-like mounds, or descend to the river bed in ranks reminiscent of Chaukundi tombs backed by mountains of magenta — the whole scene an image of absolute tranquillity in the sunlight of a flawlessly clear sky. But soon, as the channel narrows, the wall of rock rising on one side of the road, like the drop to the river bed at the other, becomes vertical. Where the river bed narrows and twists, the glowering walls of the canyon play the heavy opposite each other, giving no way. Eventually engineers had to cut a tunnel for the road inside the vertical face of the rock that stares irrevocably defiant from one side of the river into the face of the equally unyielding wall of stone that confronts it on the other.

The best times to travel through the pass are spring and autumn when the migrations to and from summer and winter grazing are on —

Above: Nomadic Baluchi family head for summer pastures with their flock of sheep.

seen and heard in the approach of a youngster on a pack camel ecstatically playing a flute in the sharp sunlit air, just for himself and his stately camel and the watching mountains and Allah who made it all so good.

History and prehistory cut paths as sharp as the river's through this pass. It was the main route to the subcontinent from Central Asia long before people used the Khyber — and for the major historic centres of Kandahar and Herat so it remains. In modern times the British used it. In 1841 when they sent troops to the first Afghan war, to defend their empire from the envy of Russia, a flash flood swept down the river bed and wiped out an entire detachment.

The road through the pass is good; but the same cannot be said of most of the driving. Like driving generally in Pakistan it's such as to make it astonishing that such a stylish, civilized, and sporting game as cricket should be Pakistan's national passion. Still, other drivers permitting, once through the Bolan Pass the traveller finds himself in no time inside the provincial capital, Quetta.

Five-and-a-half thousand feet above sea level in the Central Brahui Range, this strategically placed garrison town is the threshold of Pakistan for visitors travelling from Iran and Afghanistan. The city thus dominates access not just to the Bolan but also to the Khojak Pass which, via the border town of Chaman — 111 kilometres from Quetta (and noted for its lady-finger curry) — leads to and from Afghanistan.

In the 1980s the war in Afghanistan stopped normal overland traffic between the two countries, but ironically restored to the Khojak Pass its old strategic importance: both as an escape route for many of the millions of refugees who fled Afghanistan to settle more or less temporarily in Pakistan; and — no less vitally — as a supply line for the Mujahideen freedom fighters based just across the border inside Afghanistan.

Less often remembered today, perhaps, is that Quetta stands at the head of the roads westwards, across Baluchistan, into Iran. There are two of

Above: Group of horsemen riding through the Baluchistan desert.

these, but only the northern one, running just south of the border with Afghanistan, is a realistic option for the traveller.

It reaches Iran near Zahidan, 725 kilometres from Quetta, and is not recommended as a joy-ride — although it's but one leg of a highway that runs more than 5,000 kilometres up from Karachi and out through Zahidan and Teheran to Ankara. But to anyone interested in a day's excursion from Quetta the first stretch is highly recommended in spring as far as Nushki, 120 kilometres to the south-west, for the beauty of the highland scenery, the carpets of spring flowers and blossom-filled fruit trees, in spring splendour.

In fact, wherever there is precipitation the rugged valleys of this hardy province quickly respond, clothing themselves in great beauty. This accounts for Baluchistan's success in exporting fruit to the other provinces. It is not easily achieved. Only 3.7 per cent of the province is reckoned arable, and less than two per cent can be irrigated. Bore-drillings and tube-wells have been tried during the past two decades, but low rainfall and poor snows have lowered the water table and so disappointed expectations.

Nonetheless agriculture, the backbone of the province's economy, has developed significantly in recent years, with a wide variety among the vegetables grown — cauliflowers, beans, peas, carrots, spinach, onions, and turnips the main ones — important spring harvests of wheat and clover, and in autumn valuable yields of maize. But above all there is fruit. In spring, the road to Nushki is lovely with its promise.

Further west, however, the road shows what most of Baluchistan is made of when it meets desert, and for most of the way to the frontier then skirts the immense desolation which characterises this main block of Baluchistan. The terrible problem through all this country is lack of water.

In harsh contrast to the Quetta region, the 3,000- to 4,000-foot-high,

barren plateau that spreads across most of the region receives no smiles from nature. Naked and burning, it lies under the sun without benefit of tree cover and only the sparsest grasses to sustain the migrant flocks of goats and sheep. Most of this region, like almost half the province, sees between seven and twelve centimetres of rain a year. Most of the rest rarely has more than twenty-two centimetres.

It's been said that dry crop cultivation — in the parts where it's considered possible — is like hunting the wild ass. Still it's attempted; though experience has shown a farmer can expect no more than one full crop in five years. Even when it comes, direct rainfall is too scanty and uncertain for cultivation. The farmer must bring water from a wider catchment into the patch he judges arable. A variety of skills and much toil is brought to bear every year trying to achieve this, in the blind hope that 'this year' will produce the crop that will make the labour worthwhile.

Yet the north of the province is not the only region that has won Baluchistan its fame as Pakistan's garden. The more tropical climate in the south, behind the Makran coast, contributes significantly to Baluchistan's reputation for fruit production — mangoes, guavas, papayas, oranges, melons, water-melons, and other hot weather fruits. Dates from the Makran are justly famed for both flavour and variety. There are said to be between 100 and 150 varieties — many of them introduced by Mohamed bin Qasim in 712 when he marched his army of 12,000 through the desert that so nearly defeated Alexander the Great.

Qasim's caravans, in fact, strewed date stones along their way so generously that the route they marched can be told by the trees. The heaviest concentrations — as at Kach-Kore — show where the army stopped for food and rest. The importance of the fruit in the province today — as of the animals that doubtless bore the burden of his larder throughout bin Qasim's campaign — is reflected by the fact that Baluchis have 100 words for 'dates' — and 100 for camels.

Nevertheless, the truth about Baluchistan is that the great empty spaces and formidable mountain ranges — not to mention the fiercely independent character of its people — make most of the province a dramatic but difficult place to visit. It was too much for Cyrus the Great, very nearly broke Alexander, and showed Mohamed bin Qasim little favour. They all had somehow to cope with thorn bushes that could drag an armed man off his horse, wind-piled sandhills like bogs that their soldiers' legs sank into, searing heat by day, sharp cold at night, no water — and then, off distant hills, flash floods that could wipe out entire companies of men. Not what anyone could call hospitable terrain.

Quetta is quite different — an established and increasingly popular tourist region, especially during the spring months.

It pretends to no beauty as a city. Whatever remained of the settlement taken by Mahmud of Ghazni in the eleventh century, the township defended by the Mughals against Persian incursions in the sixteenth and occupied by the British under Sir Robert Sandeman in the last quarter of the nineteenth century, an earthquake practically annihilated in the early hours of 31 May, 1935. Twenty-four thousand people — some say half as many again — perished. The city was re-built mainly in bungalow or two-floor style, on a grid plan. The streets are wide and pleasant with trees. There is a University and a famous military Staff College.

What will probably most impress the visitor arriving in Quetta from Sibi is the capital's cool. Its lofty situation — the word Quetta is said to have grown from the Pushtoo word Kot (fort) — means that the drive of a few hours can have brought you through 30°, even 40° C. By any standards that's a cold shower and seriously invigorating. 'Happy are they who live in Quetta from May to August', declares a guide book. Indeed. But the writer neglects to mention the other eight months when, of course, the cool, jasmine-scented breeze gives way to something appreciably sterner, and vigorous young men bundle heavy woollen blankets round themselves and huddle out of the scythe-like blast under their broad, flat loden-style hats, close by blazing wood fires.

Such sharp conditions doubtless account for the look of enviable rude health worn by the the city's mainly Pathan population. All the same, robust health notwithstanding, those who visit Quetta in say February may well find themselves muttering, again and again, those so well chosen words of the guide book: 'Happy are they . . . from May to August . . . .'

Quetta's bazaars take pride in their handicraft products — Baluchi mirror-work embroidery, intricately designed carpets, jackets, waistcoats, fur coats, and sandals. The old bazaars offer local delicacies, such as the *sajji* — barbecued leg of lamb — and *landhi* — whole lamb dried in shade and kept for winter. But above all it is with their mountains of seasonal fruit that the bazaars of Quetta distinguish themselves.

Even in this most favoured part of the province rainfall does not spoil the farmers. At most it's thirty centimetres, and, as everwhere in Baluchistan, it's unreliable. But Quetta-area farmers enjoy a double advantage over their struggling compatriots elsewhere in the province. The high mountain surroundings trap moisture. It may fall as snow, but there's always enough of it to irrigate their fields and valley holdings. Secondly, the railway link gets their produce to assured markets in Karachi, Hyderabad, and Multan.

The result is that the valleys surrounding the provincial capital, literally covered with fruit trees — apples, apricots, pomegranates, peaches, plums,pears, cherries, quinces, almonds, walnuts, pistachios, musk-melons, water melons, figs, and grapes — are lovely to visit in spring. Generally the trees are short-trunked and espaliered. However grown, they thrive.

By early May the produce has begun to appear in the markets: cherries first, then apricots, then grapes and peaches — the big and luscious Sanfroza are famous — then apples, and so on. Fruit has been called Quetta's cash crop. It's exported all over the country.

Yet it isn't the only thing that grows around Quetta. In the spring, after the rains, the countryside is green with grasses too, and soon studded with red and yellow tulips, wild hyacinths, irises of all colours, and carmine poppies. Then, till the June harvest, the fields are transformed into a rolling sea of waving cornfields. Trees of all kinds flourish — in particular large forests of ephedra, from which the drug ephedrine, used for asthma, is manufactured. In the city too, flowers of all kinds are cultivated. Quetta is famous for its roses and rose-water.

Quetta is the key to many valleys of outstanding natural beauty —

Opposite: An Afghan shoemaker, one of many millions of refugees who sought shelter in Pakistan from the bitter decade-long civil war in Afghanistan, plies his trade in a Quetta street.

Opposite left: Two Pathan merchants in the shade of their Quetta shop.

Opposite: Smiling Pathan, one of the majority communities in Baluchistan, with beard deftly rejuvenated by touches of henna.

especially in spring. All are fruit-fertile and cool, and many are also culturally or otherwise interesting: one for the presence of some rare, threatened species of animal, for example, and another for some culinary speciality; the Chautar Valley, for its houses built with juniper bark — quite unlike the everywhere-else mud huts; and all the hills about Quetta itself because they are said to be inhabited by descendants of Genghis Khan.

Most popular of all the area's resorts is the hill-station of Ziarat — nestling 8,200 feet above sea level, 132 kilometres east-north-east of Quetta, in the midst of one of the largest and oldest juniper forests in the world. Some of these great, but slow-growing trees are said to be 5,000 years old. The sap, found like stray tears on the bole, tastes like a liquid definition of the word 'pungent'.

Ziarat's name — which means 'Shrine' — refers to Kharwari Baba, a holy man who rested in the valley and was buried there after his death. The great Muslim feast of Eid at his shrine in the hills eight kilometres from Ziarat town is celebrated with wrestling and other sports.

Favoured among holiday-makers above all for its enchanting situation,

Above: Museum mortar-piece stands outside the former home of Britain's World War II hero, Field Marshal Bernard Montgomery, a distinguished prewar alumnus of Quetta's Military Staff College.

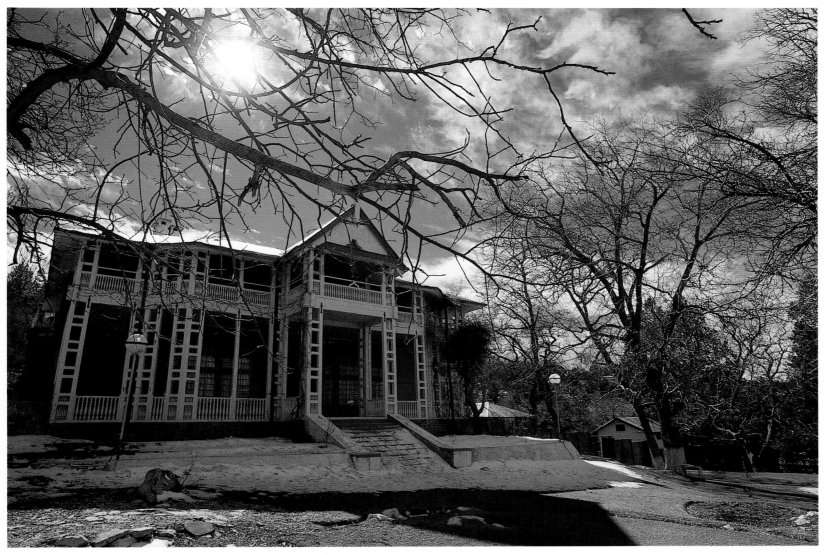

Above: Winter snow still lies in the shadows of the Ziarat residency, Baluchistan, where Quaid-i-Azam, Mohamed Ali Jinnah, spent his last days before his death in 1948.

Ziarat offers the idyllic combination of superb views, and refreshingly cool heights to enjoy them in, even in the hottest summer. In spring, walking and climbing are especially popular because of the ever wider-ranging, often breathtaking views of the surrounding valleys and the flowered and forested hills. But winter is cold and the road is often closed by snow.

Quaid-i-Azam, Mohamed Ali Jinnah was particularly fond of Ziarat. He spent his last days in the Governor's Residency there. This attractive two-storey rest house is set in a fine, beautifully-lawned garden with a superb prospect over the valley. For many visitors it has become almost a shrine.

A feature of this region is the *karez* — a system of tunnels that brings shallow groundwater to the surface where it can irrigate fields on the flanks of hills. The excavation and maintenance of the tunnels is an expert and dangerous job, generally undertaken by Brahui tribesmen.

Some *karez* occur naturally, when narrow openings in the mountainside allow the groundwater to issue from the rocks — with visually pleasing and often dramatic waterfall effects. The gorges, or

tangi, they make are popular with hikers and picnickers.

Among the half-dozen around Ziarat, Sandeman Tangi — named after Sir Robert Sandeman, commissioner for the district in 1866 before he was appointed political agent — is perhaps the favourite.

Ninety-five kilometres north-east of the provincial capital, hidden by barren hills of multi-coloured rock, runs the little-known but spectacularly lovely, 320-kilometre-long Zhob Valley — home of another of Pakistan's yet-to-be-revealed ancient cultures. It is also — in one of those striking conjunctions of old and new with which all Pakistan abounds — the centre, in Muslimbagh, of the country's strategically important chromite mining industry.

Never less than 4,500 feet above sea level, and enclosed by 10,000-foot-high hills (or mountains, as they'd be called anywhere else) the Zhob Valley abounds in fruit, wild flowers, trees — and history. Certainly flourishing on the ancient caravan routes into Afghanistan in 3,000 BC, agricultural communities which may yet be found to rival Mehr Gahr as the oldest on the subcontinent produced earthenware goods that link them with the great Bronze Age cultures of Iran and Mesopotamia. The

Above: Over the centuries earthquakes of stunning intensity have created many fissures in the rocky landscape of Baluchistan, including well-known Sandeman's Tangi, near Ziarat, named after a British proconsul of 1866.

pottery, by contrast, suggests links with the Indus Valley civilization that followed.

Various tribes of Kakar Pathans live in the Zhob Valley. They are medium-height, well-built people, mostly wheat-complexioned, but some really fair and blue eyed. Their hospitality is famous — the coming of a guest is counted a blessing. This is the home of *landhi* — the slowly pole-dried and salted strips of specially fattened sheep. Green tea is the favourite drink.

Most often the women wear red, said to date from an era when the various tribes spent much time shooting firearms at each other but did not want to hit women.

Despite long contact with the world outside the valley many other ancient traditions are maintained. One, which seems to hold the potential for the most grievous frustration, requires the bridegroom's party to defeat the bride's in marksmanship before the groom can take his new wife to his house.

The way down from Quetta to the Indus Valley is long and not easy by road — dramatically beautiful as much of the harshly-eroded landscape is. The approach to Dera Ghazi Khan, especially, is spectacularly steep.

But for most travellers the Bolan route is advised, and for those who want something different from the road up, the train offers an agreeable alternative. Quetta's railway station, still used by steam locomotives, is practically a monument to that bygone and perhaps more colourful age. In its more than 5,000-foot descent the track cuts through twenty dramatic tunnels. The views are superb and the ride smooth. If you can get a sleeper it's a stylish way to leave this garden in the wilderness.

> *'Man has fortune of his own'*
> — Motto on Punjab truck

In 1933 a group of undergraduates studying at Cambridge University, England, produced a pamphlet entitled 'Now or Never'. The booklet backed the idea of a separate Muslim state in the old Indian subcontinent and proposed that its name, as well as its territory, should be based on the Muslim majority regions in the north-west.

Both the idea of the new state and the proposed name won acceptance — hence 'Pakistan', with P for Punjab, A (for the Afghanistan border area of North-West Frontier Province) K for Kashmir, S for Sind and Baluchi*stan*. The name had more significance for a state that was intended to shepherd together the people of one religious faith. In Urdu — the future state's national language — *Pakistan* means Land of the Pure.

Whether by accident or design, it's fitting that Punjab should be the first province represented in the country's name. More than half of Pakistan's teeming millions live there, and economically it's by far the most developed area of the country, with many agricultural, commercial, and industrial centres within its borders.

This economic pre-eminence is no quirk of post-Independence development. As with the other two great river valley systems that were life-blood to prehistoric man's civilizations, the Nile and the Tigris-Euphrates, the economic potential of the great Indus plain and its tributaries was recognised by man at least 5,000 years ago. Punjab takes its name — it means Five Rivers — from the Indus tributaries, the Jhelum, Chenab, Ravi, Sutlej, and Beas. They, and even more the fabled Indus to which they pay their tribute, nourish the agricultural wealth which remains the basis of Punjab's prosperity.

Modern man has enhanced the natural strength of the region with the largest — and many consider the finest — irrigation scheme in the world. The Sukkur barrage in Sind, the first of several established on the Indus itself and on its tributaries, was part of a grand plan, now achieved, to link the rivers by canals, and so guarantee irrigation for most of the Punjab and much of Sind.

To a great extent it was Independence that shaped the system. The acrimony that attended the division of old India was at its most bitter — outside the three wars that have taken place — with regard to Pakistan's water requirement. The problem arose because the Indus and nearly all its tributaries flowed through the new India, or Indian-held land, before entering Pakistan and were thus subject to Indian control.

After India shut off the Ravi and the Sutlej — with disastrous consequences for Pakistan's crops — international arbitration was invoked. Eventually, this led to the 1960 settlement which gave Pakistan the three western rivers — the Indus, the Jhelum, and the Chenab — and India the three eastern rivers. During an agreed transition period, Pakistan built a canal network with international help, to transfer water from 'its' rivers to those areas formerly supplied by the Ravi and Sutlej (the Beas River — an important part of the pre-Partition Punjab system — joins the Sutlej before the border created in 1947 and is thus exclusively an Indian river).

Enormous dams — at Tarbela on the Indus and at Mangla on the Jhelum — were built to ensure year-round water availability. The vast, integrated irrigation system this created ranks as the most complex and

Previous pages: Camel treads a lonely circle turning a traditional irrigation water-wheel to tap the Indus and bring a flush of green to a peasant smallholding.

Opposite: Mustard ripening in the background, a Punjab farmer happily surveys his burgeoning smallholding.

Opposite: Boys and buffaloes cool off in the torrid heat of a Punjab summer.

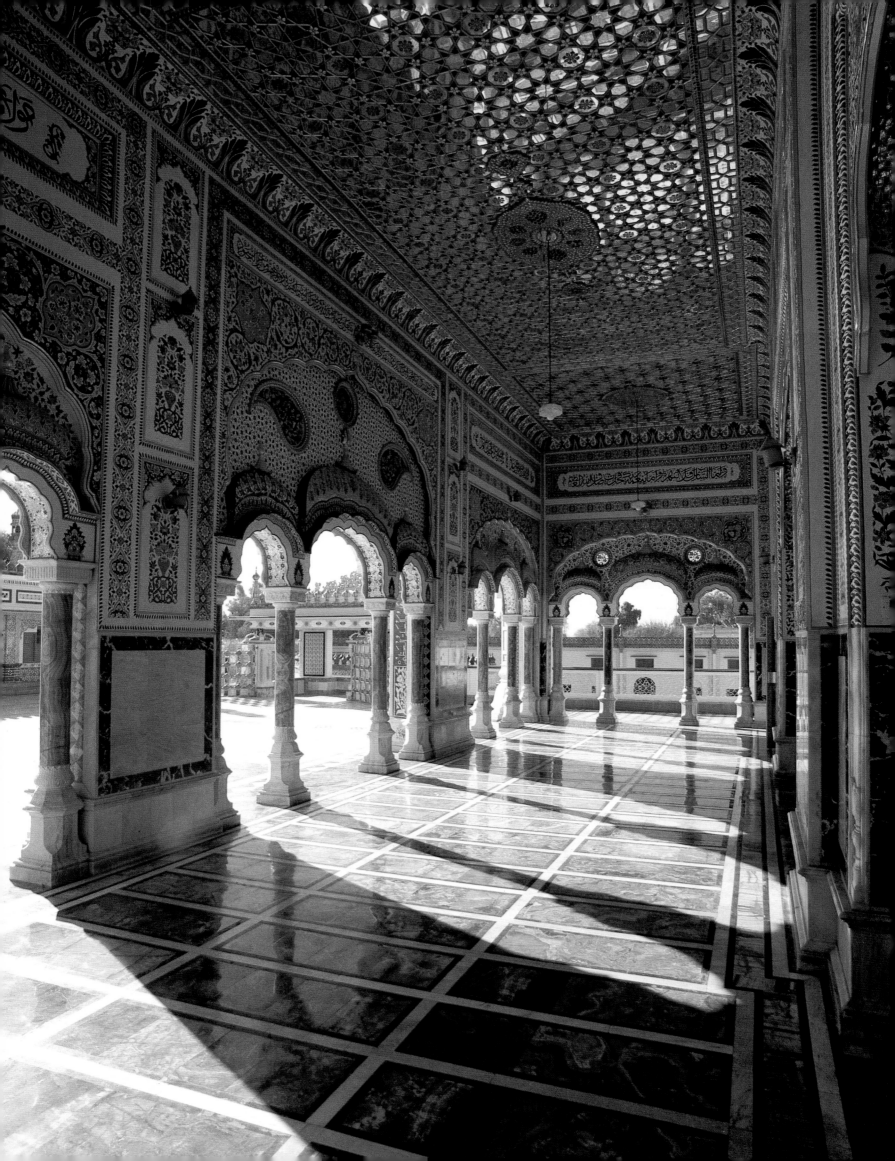

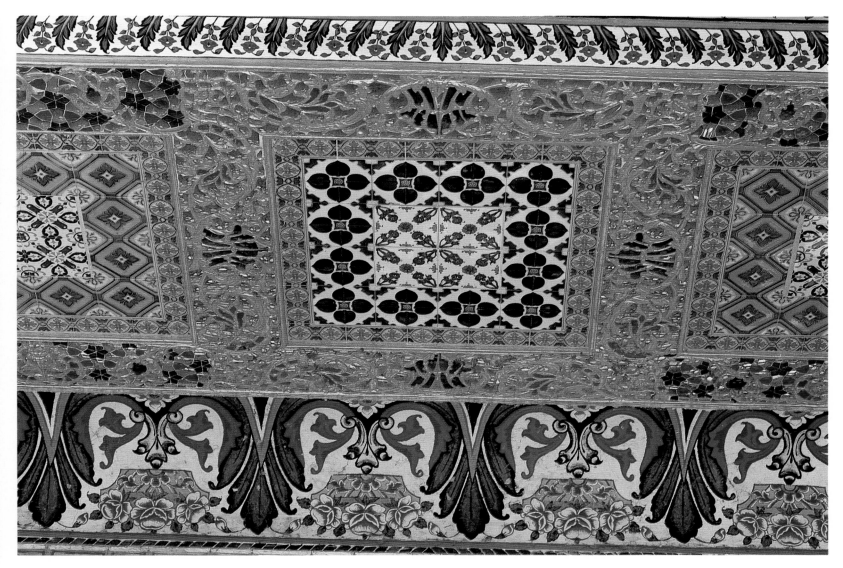

Above: Floral and geometric inlays crown the ceiling of Bhong mosque with multi-coloured splendour.

Right: Rich royal blue on white ceramics adorn the stunning minaret of Bhong mosque.

Opposite: Soft spring sun casts gleaming shadows across the polished floor of Pakistan's 'fairy-tale prettiest' mosque — at Bhong in southern Punjab.

extensive in the long history of mankind's adaptation of natural water resources to agricultural need. But it is no luxury. It was vital to maintain and secure the Punjab's agricultural strength.

No more vivid indication of the province's importance could be given than the regret of Sher Shah Suri in 1545. No mean soldier, on his deathbed this Afghan usurper of the Mughal throne lamented that he had never destroyed Lahore, the Pearl of the Punjab, and inevitably — because of its situation in the middle of the plain — at once extremely wealthy and excessively vulnerable.

Such a prize, the Shah believed, was impossible to make impregnable, must always tempt invaders, and provide them with all they needed to equip their way to further ravages across the subcontinent. Better it had been laid waste . . . .

Lahore was not destroyed. Too often, though — as Sher Shah Suri had foreseen — like the rest of Punjab, it was attacked, pillaged, and raped. And so, traditionally peaceful farmers, the Punjabis gradually acquired necessary traditions of self-defence. Both the ancient and the more recent traditions endure to this day. Punjab still provides the bulk of Pakistan's

Above: Though undermined and fragmented by the floodwaters of the Chenab and Sutlej rivers, the glory that was Uchh Sharif's as a leading religious and cultural centre of Islam lingers on in the haunting ruins of the once magnificent 'Domes of the Saints'.

Above: Painted ceiling of the ancient shrine to the Uchh Sharif saint.

twentieth-century economic strength, and also most of the personnel in the country's highly professional armed forces.

Twenty-four kilometres up the road from the Sind-Punjab border, a turnoff towards the Indus leads to Bhong and one of the fairy-tale-prettiest, and most lavishly-decorated mosques you could ever wish to see. In the tranquillity of the countryside only five kilometres from the river, under an almost overwhelming intricacy of gold leaf decoration and bold colour, the mosque basks in sunshine on a raised platform that carries it like some fantastically-ornamented 'magic carpet'. The six mainly white minars, dazzling under the sun, are complemented by the white marble, striped with black, of the elevated courtyard. The use of marble throughout, but particularly the green-, brown-, and carmine-veined stone of the mosque pillars and floor, is most effective. An outstanding feature of the decoration is the calligraphy.

Built in the 1960's by local landlord Rais Ghazi Shabir, the mosque is already famous for its splendour. In 1986 it won the coveted Aga Khan award for mosque architecture. The conjunction of beauty, artistry, and wealth in the service of faith, set aside here so near, but still so far away from the hurlyburly of the twentieth-century highway, is a reminder that for all its ambitions, achievements, and problems, ultimately Pakistan, and its greatest resources, are all about faith — the creed that makes it one.

Back amid the tumult of traffic on the road north, 'I love you but you don't want me', laments the rear of the truck in front. For nearly ten minutes — doubtless desperate with unrequited love — the driver has been taking his life in his hands in vain attempts to get away but the bulbous, bugling bus in front of his lorry absolutely refuses to yield pole position. Neither of them seems to have seen that other legend inscribed on the truck in Karachi, 'Live, my child!'

The 'bons mots' on Pakistan's vehicles humanise what's often otherwise an alarmingly mechanical and utterly reckless race of overloaded, top-heavy, multi-wheeled, claxon-tooting giants that, for all the poetry blazoned across them, more often than not demonstrate their single-minded dedication to a bleaker philosophy: 'Do or die'. Even Pakistan's official tourism directory warns that 'driving can be hazardous', deftly adding that, 'few people care to follow the traffic rules meticulously.' Words are indeed wonderful things.

'Non-meticulous' driving is not the only hazard. The roads themselves, in northern Sind and southern Punjab especially, are under constant and heavy pressure of traffic. They suffer in consequence, adding a measure of tension to what otherwise must be the best way to see this so varied country.

Not that travellers coming into Punjab from Sind — once Bhong's been visited — have very much to distract attention from the wheels pounding under and around their vehicle. The provincial border country is hard by the north-westerly bulge of the quarter-million-square-kilometre Thar desert which, with the Rann of Kutch to the south, has always set the Indus Valley people an uncompromising eastern limit to where they could settle.

Nowadays the Thar reaches into 26,000 square kilometres of Pakistan. It is called, ominously, the Cholistan — from a word which means, in a reference to the shifting dunes, 'walking'. In Alexander the Great's time this dune-land was watered by the now dried-up river Ghaggar. Long before Alexander's army passed this way, literally hundreds of ancient settlements flourished along its banks, many belonging to the Harappa-Moenjodaro empire. But, even for an Indus Valley expert, little remains to get excited about.

The next point of interest is eighty kilometres upriver from Bhong, where the Indus receives, in a single confluence, the tribute of all five of Punjab's ancient waterways.

Almost as if unwilling to approach the mighty Indus separately the five tributaries have been coming together, gradually, for the last 500 kilometres. Beas has already joined forces with the Sutlej before the latter crossed the international border with India; then, in Pakistan, first the Jhelum, and then the Ravi, combined with the Chenab while it was still only halfway down its course through the Punjab. Flowing on then in just two courses — Sutlej and Chenab — the five rivers finally become one in a single tributary, the Panjnad, seventy kilometres north of where this delivers the mingled waters of them all to the Indus.

Above: Redolent with the pomp and circumstance of the age of empire, this embellished gateway to the palace of the princely rulers of Bahawalpur took three years to build, from 1882 to 1885.

Given the importance of the rivers to the country you may feel this final union calls for celebration — if only a toast in tea. But there's nothing. No town, not even a bridge; only a ferry links the east-bank and west-bank highways.

But at the final confluence of the Punjab Five — where the Chenab joins the Sutlej — it's quite different. On a plateau some eleven kilometres from the confluence stands Uchh Sharif, a city of ancient renown.

Impossible to date, the foundation of Uchh is variously said to be 'at least a century before Christ' and by others attributed to Alexander the Great in 325 BC. Some say a city stood here long before Alexander. They identify it with that city which sent him 100 hostages of noble birth and 500 war chariots — horsed and manned and fully armed — as a pledge of welcome. By that time, Alexander had done a lot of fighting — every inch of the way, it seems, across the *doabs* between the five rivers — and was now sailing south only because his troops refused to go beyond the Beas. The offering of the people of ancient Uchh — if Uchh it was — pleased the western warlord. He sent the

Opposite: Bahawalpur potter hand paints a piece before firing, using designs handed down from generation to generation, although within the tradition the decoration of every pot differs.

Above: A slowly dying craft as more and more craftsmen are lured abroad to better paid jobs in the Gulf states, pottery remains a staple Bahawalpur industry. The craftsman who remain spin and shape as many as twenty-five vessels a day.

hostages home. But, good professional, he kept the chariots.

Whatever the truth about its origins, Uchh is certainly of pre-Islamic foundation. In AD 712, after a seven-day siege, it fell to Mohamed bin Qasim — a small mosque in the town is said to have been built by him — and in the following centuries attracted scholars and saints from as far off as Baghdad and Bukhara. By the thirteenth century, Uchh had achieved renown as a University city famous for its many shrines.

Proximity to the rivers — which doubtless brought the first settlers to the site, whenever that was — has unfortunately entailed penalties for the many superb buildings erected here in those centuries of glory. Floods have undermined many of them. Nonetheless, for what remains, as well as for its past religious and cultural importance, Uchh rewards a visit.

The group of tombs known as the 'Domes of the Saints' suffered quite grievously from flooding, but nonetheless that of Mai Javindi — a saintly woman who died in 1403 — remains outstandingly beautiful. Built in 1498 it shows — like all the tombs in this group — the strong central Asian influence evident in the great Rukn-e-Alam mausoleum that is the glory of Multan and on which they are all obviously modelled. The blue mosaic so characteristic of all the great buildings from Thatta to Multan decks the massive solidity of the design with a cool confidence that remains astonishingly intact even though one half of the building has gone, destroyed when the foundations were washed away.

In total contrast, nearby, is the shrine of the twelfth-century saint, Surkh Bukhari, a brick and stone building with carved wooden pillars that support a decorated wooden ceiling across the sixty-bay interior. Tinsel and coloured string flowers are strung from pillar to pillar over the many tombs to provide a touch of piety in this dark, slightly forbidding interior. The shrine is a popular complement to the classic dignity of the 'Domes of the Saints'.

Seventy-seven kilometres north of Uchh, and less than a kilometre short of the river Sutlej, spreads the once princely state of Bahawalpur. This pleasingly-relaxed, clean-looking, wide-open city of boulevards and impressive modern buildings has its own memories of a pre-Independence independence. Like Uchh, Bahawalpur lacks records of its origins but these are assumed to be pre-Islamic. With the coming of Islam it was ruled by governors appointed by the Caliphs of Damascus and Baghdad; indeed many of its rulers claimed descent from an uncle of the Prophet.

In 1748 the Abbasi family founded the modern princely state. They were confirmed in power under a treaty with the British in 1833 and ruled until 1954, when the independent state merged with Pakistan.

The ancestral seat of these Amirs is Derawar Fort, in the Cholistan desert. Closer to Bahawalpur, at Dera Nawab Sahib, are the modern palaces, chief of which is Sadiq Garh, built between 1882 and 1885. This proudly-gated palace on a country road has such presence that it conjures in the mind images of flags, bugles, and drums, stunningly-smart soldiers in dress uniforms and crisply exact in their drill, and thoughts of a social order and way of life now utterly alien even to the land from which they came. Nevertheless, while they lasted, they

possessed that undeniable quality that can only be called, however inadequately, style.

Above: Nomadic family shape colourful paper flowers to eke a living.

That same quality is much in evidence in the crafts fostered in the modern city. These include traditional carpet weaving, using a basis of string to support the locally-produced cotton weave, shoe embroidery, and pottery. Shoe-making, in bead-decorated, cloth-covered leather, caters to practical daily need as well as to ceremonial occasions such as marriage and the Eid congregational prayers. For the latter, the shoes or slippers will be splendidly-worked with silver thread; the former will be made pretty with plastic beads. The basic design of all the footwear — turned up and pointed or curled like the prow of a boat — is distinctively Bahawalpuri.

The locally-made pottery also remains faithful to traditional styles — though, within the tradition, the decoration of every single pot is individual.

This university city has a number of other senior educational institutions, among them the modern but already well-established Quaid-i-Azam Medical College. It is also well-endowed with leisure

Opposite: Lush harvest of fruit from Punjab's fertile orchards finds a ready market in the province's fast-growing capital of Lahore.

facilities, from a fine cricket ground to a twenty-eight-square-kilometre national park at Lal Suhanra, forty kilometres to the east. This is so close to the Cholistan desert that the thick forest each side of the Bahawal canal, and the natural lake, come as a surprise. The trees and water provide a habitat for many species of birds, including peacocks, partridges, kingfishers, quails, pheasants, falcons, and, of course, parrots; as well as a wide range of desert and forest animals, from the abundant wild boar to the rare chinkara gazelle.

And then, 106 kilometres further north, across the Sutlej and close to the Chenab, stands Multan — according to some, the oldest living city in south Asia.

Indeed Multan features in many ancient tales, including one that tells how, when Adam and Eve and Satan were expelled from Eden, Multan is where the last-named landed. If this story is designed to explain the origins of the city's well-founded reputation for intolerable summer heat it has a rival — one in which a holy man, being flayed alive in the city, called upon the sun to avenge him.

Dust, beggars, and burial grounds are other things Multan is reputed

Above: An incredible bedlam of noise and colour, Pakistan's traffic symbolises all the vibrant, nonstop energy and enterprise of the nation, with entrepreneurial bus operators improvising upper decks out of the baggage roof of their single-deck vehicles.

Opposite: Horse drawn victorias, or tongas, remain a cheap and popular choice of transport in Lahore and other cities and towns throughout the land.

Above: Curious child stares out from inside a bus.

to abound with; and it may be allowed that the city has its share of each. But none of this should discourage the visitor. Multan is a shrine of history, culture, and religion.

Scholars seem to agree that Multan is that capital city of the fierce warrior tribe of Mallians where Alexander the Great was grievously, perhaps in the end lethally, wounded. Literally leading the attack, as was his wont, the Macedonian emperor had jumped down from the city wall — which he and three followers alone had succeeded in scaling — onto a mound thick with the enemy.

In the middle of the fierce hand-to-hand fighting that followed Alexander was pierced in the chest by a metre-long arrow. It penetrated one of his lungs and it seems he never fully recovered, though thanks to the extraordinary strength of his physique he reached Baghdad — despite the ghastly ordeal of crossing the Makran desert without supplies — before dying, apparently from a bout of malaria, some time later.

Multan too is where, 1,000 years after Fate began to curb Alexander's meteor-like progress, the young Muslim hero Mohamed bin Qasim halted in his progress up the Indus Valley. He didn't know it at the time but writing was on the wall for him as well.

He had sent the Caliph, for his harem, two beautiful girls whose Hindu Raja father he had killed. In revenge, one of the girls told the Caliph in Damascus that bin Qasim had raped her before sending her to him. In fury at the insult, the Caliph immediately ordered bin Qasim to be sewn alive into a raw cowhide and sent back home — a terrible death as the hide slowly contracts; in effect not unlike the later English practice of pressing people to death between a sharp stone and huge weights heaped on a door on top. When bin Qasim's body reached Damascus the girls gloated — admitting the young general's innocence. They were immediately beheaded.

Before bin Qasim brought Islam to the country, the Chinese Buddhist traveller Hsuan Tsang visited Multan. That was about AD 640. He found the city pleasing and prosperous. At that time, religion was predominantly spirit-worship, and Hsuan described in some detail a temple dedicated to the sun with an image cast in gold and embedded with rare stones. No trace of the temple remains — Aurangzeb, the last of the great Mughal emperors and a devout Muslim, is said to have destroyed it 1,000 years after Hsuan's visit.

Reflecting the haphazard fortunes of the city and all the surrounding country through the centuries known in Europe as the Dark and the Middle Ages, Multan fell to the Afghan Mahmud of Ghazni in 1005 and to the Mongol Tamurlane in 1398.

In 1528 the founder of the Mughal dynasty, Babur, assumed control, bringing an era of peace and prosperity under which the city thrived until the middle of the eighteenth century. A hundred years of turmoil and a succession of rulers — Persian, Afghan, and Sikh — finally brought the city under British rule in 1849.

Multan was never a pushover. Having half-killed Alexander the Great, and held Mohamed bin Qasim at bay for two months before he could enter, it repulsed the British through six long months. The battle ended only after the British had destroyed most of the ancient citadel fort which

was the mainstay of the resistance. Much reduced from its former two-and-a-half kilometre circumference, the fort still commands the heights of the city and provides the best, panoramic view.

The layout has much in common with Pakistan's other truly ancient cities: Hyderabad in Sind, Lahore further north in Punjab, and Peshawar in the North-West Frontier Province. As with those others, the early nucleus is easily recognisable in the cluster of lanes and alleyways that serve the warren-like congestion of the 'old city'. This is dominated, as in Hyderabad, Lahore, and Peshawar, by the remains of the ancient fort.

Outside this older area, again like those others, Multan shows the regular rectilinear layout of the typical British cantonment where administrators, army depots, and hospitals were, and still are, located. In between these two — the old city and the cantonment — are sited those monuments of civil administration, the law courts, municipal offices, and regional branches of higher administrative bodies like the irrigation department. Elsewhere, outside the old city area, are found the larger units of modern industry. Post-independence housing suburbs occupy yet other sectors.

But it's in the old city, close to the fort's main gate, that Multan's glory

Above: Bahawalpur craftsmen weave a traditional carpet in an intricate design that uses string for the warp and cotton for the weft. The carpet will take three weeks to complete.

Above: Traditional Lahore craft carpets, handwoven from centuries-old designs, can fetch as much as 30,000 dollars on the American market.

— and surely one of Pakistan's greatest — is to be found. The fourteenth-century mausoleum of Shah Rukn-ud-Din, also known as Rukn-e-Alam, is an awesome achievement. Built of brick between 1320 and 1324, it descends in three stages. The hemispherical dome — eighteen metres in diameter — rests on an octagon, turreted at the corners, that expands as it descends. This in turn is borne on a greater octagon, widest at ground level, whose corners are secured with sloped, spherical towers which are also turreted and, like the walls, widest at the base.

The power of the design is immense. Even the Mughals never surpassed its grandeur.

And the decoration is worthy of the design. The warmth of the dark-red bricks is variously, and discreetly enhanced by contrasting blue, azure, white, and turquoise tiles, mosaics, calligraphy, and colourful floral and geometric devices. Inside, the flush of the bricks about the lovely dome blends superbly with the blue of the tile inlay.

The Rukn-ud-Din mausoleum was built by a Tughlaq king for himself but the ruler's son ordered it handed over for the burial of Rukn-ud-Din — an eminent scholar of enormous political and religious influence. He was related to another greatly revered religious leader, Hazrat Baha-ud-

Above: Followers pay homage in the Multan shrine of the mausoleum of Bahi-udin-Zakria and his son.

Opposite: The majestic proportions of the fourteenth-century mausoleum of the famous Multan scholar, Shah Rukn-ud din, is one of the most powerful of all Mughal monuments.

Din Zakaria, whose own tomb is nearby. This Sheikh — a thirteenth-century sufi — travelled widely before settling in Multan. His mausoleum, likewise of imposing proportions, suffered quite badly in the 1848 siege.

Besides its numerous shrines, Multan is noted as a stronghold of ancient handicrafts, especially handloom weaving, pottery, glazed tiles, and camel skin products. These last include surely one of the least expected lines: lamp-shades — often elaborately and most delicately-painted in traditional floral and geometric patterns.

Multan is practically in the middle of Pakistan, and the roads north cut through increasingly fertile tracts of country. This is that ancient Punjab, the land of the Five Rivers, whose alluvial deposits and the crops they grew brought down upon the hard-working farmers that endless-seeming sequence of marauders and more serious invaders that is the despair of modern students.

Fortunately the details of these successive waves of ransackers and settlers are not required reading for visitors. But it helps understanding of this remarkable country to peruse what's effectively just a list of the

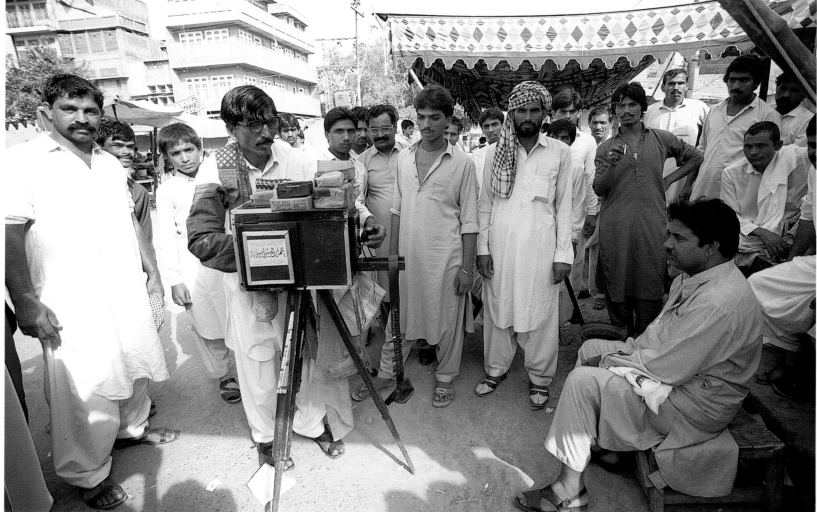

Opposite: Dressed in rich silks and brocades, guests and family prepare for a Lahore wedding.

129

Above: Artist works on traditional lampshade made of camel leather.

main chapter headings under which the many different intruders entered the Punjab: from the prehistoric founders of the Indus Valley civilization, through the Aryans from central Asia (around 1700 BC) who are believed to have caused or contributed to the decline of Moenjodaro and Harappa, the Persians and Macedonians who followed them, then the Mauryans and Bactrian Greeks, the Scythians and Parthians, Kushans and Sassanians and White Huns, the Turks from Afghanistan, Arabs from the Gulf under Mohamed bin Qasim, Ghaznivids and Ghorids again from Afghanistan, Mongols under Ghengis Khan, and Turks and others under Tamurlane, Mughals led by Babur, Nadir Shah's Persians, Ahmad Shah Durrani's Afghans, Ranjit Singh's Sikhs, and the last century's British.

It was the crops of the Punjab that grounded the wealth of all the many kingdoms and empires that were established on the subcontinent, long before the assiduous use of irrigation which has characterised development through most of the past century and a half.

Thus, driving northwards from Multan and seeing the twentieth-century's harvest — the vast, unfeatured fields of wheat, rice, cotton, and sugarcane, and the urbanisation and industrialisation it has encouraged in centres like Multan, Faisalabad, Lahore, Gujranwala, Sialkot, and Gujrat — you are also looking at the reason for this enormous river basin's tempestuous history. All through the ages it was agricultural wealth that lured invaders into this fabulous valley.

Today the enemy of this natural wealth is different, but as great a preoccupation for good government. You do not drive long without seeing the white crust on the surface that betrays waterlogging and deadening salinity. It's estimated it renders 400 kilometres of land a year infertile. Simply containing the problem is a constant battle. And as was mentioned in connection with Moenjodaro's remains, the saturation of the ground with water is having a disastrous effect there. It's a cruel reminder of Harappa's devastation.

In 1856, when the British were building a railway line from Multan to Lahore, the engineer-in-charge discovered — to his astonishment and delight — an immense buried brickyard. He had found, virtually *in situ*, the ballast he needed for the track he must build. Nearly half the estimated available total of bricks had been used before the horrendous realisation dawned.

Most of 160 kilometres of railway line was by then standing on the 4,500-year-old remains of a previously unknown civilization. A great city — contemporary with, quite different from, and in many ways vastly superior to those of the Pharaohs on the Nile and Mesopotamia's Twin River kingdoms — had been dug up, to make a bed for a track for trains.

The realisation stopped the use of Harappa as a quarry. But serious excavation of the site had to wait until the discovery, in 1922, of Moenjodaro — nearly 800 kilometres to the south-west. Striking similarities between the two immediately became clear — first in the artefacts, such as seals and painted pottery, then in the actual layout.

Although the River Ravi today flows several kilometres to the north it was clear that originally Harappa, too, was a riverside city, built on the Ravi's southern bank. Like Moenjodaro, too, Harappa was upwards of five kilometres in circumference and consisted of two parts: a lofty citadel mound and the lower but much more extensive remains east of it.

Opposite: Faisalabad street photographer, using homemade camera complete with its own 'polaroid' instant developer inside, carefully times his exposure.

Below: The buried remains of one of the world's oldest cities were plundered for ballast in the middle of the last century by a railway contractor unaware that he had stumbled upon the ruins of Harappa, the twin city state to Moenjodaro in the Indus Valley Civilization that flourished more than 4,500 years ago.

Above: Street musician, Punjab.

Opposite left: Steatite seal from the Indus Valley Civilization of Moenjodaro and Harappa with tantalizing hieroglyphics to which no key has yet been found.

Opposite: Elephant and other wildlife were common symbols on the steatite seals used by the Indus Valley Civilization's revenue men to identify the goods of individual traders.

Close to the old river bed was the same remarkable granary complex found in Moenjodaro.

Although the site was almost destroyed by the railway quarrying, making it difficult to establish the actual plan of the residential area so clear at Moenjodaro, the individual structures are of the same burnt brick, there are the same covered drains down the roads, identical pottery design and decoration, and — most characteristic of the Indus Valley products — steatite seals. It was very quickly realised that Harappa and Moenjodaro were sister cities.

Unlike Moenjodaro, Harappa yielded some of the secrets of its own background. The British archaeologist Sir Mortimer Wheeler tells how efforts to get at the Sind city's origins were frustrated. Digging in the driest season of the year, they struck water five metres below the present surface. With the help of mechanised pumps and careful engineering, the team dived a further three metres into the streaming mud. 'Then one night, when the inadequate pumps were still labouring, a thousand jets of water burst from the sides of our cutting, and with a sullen roar it tumbled in . . . time and tide had beaten us.'

At Harappa, they were luckier. After penetrating fifteen metres down in the suffocatingly-hot dry season they reached within a small area 'the beginning of things' in the shape of a short-lived village culture lying on the natural surface of the ground beneath the citadel of the later city. Harappa has also revealed preliminary stages of the city's evolution: strikingly reminiscent of what was discovered at Kot Diji and Amri in Sind.

As at Moenjodaro there is a noticeable lack of weapons. Were armaments banned by the dominant Citadel class for fear of overthrow? Or because of a natural pacificism? As at Moenjodaro, there seems to have been a decline in material prosperity towards the end of the city's occupation. River flooding, too, was clearly a permanent hazard. But just why Harappa's elaborate civilization ended is unknown.

Work on the as yet undeciphered Indus Valley Script continues. It could perhaps reveal the answer. The problem is that the Indus Valley has yielded no such thing as the Rosetta Stone which gave the clue to the meaning of ancient Egyptian hieroglyphs. It also seems that much, if not all, of what was written was by way of personal identification, and being individual cannot be compared with other examples to establish regular patterns. All known examples are very short, too. None has more than seventeen letters. It gives an expert little to go on. Harappa is dated from 2500-1800 BC, again, like Moenjodaro, on the basis of the evidence of commercial exchanges with Mesopotamia, where the chronology is more easily established.

Two more places in the region deserve mention. Pakpattan, on the Sutlej, is thought to have been home to one of the tribes which caused Alexander trouble in the fourth century BC, during his journey southward. In the thirteenth century, it was home to an eminent dervish scholar whose feast day still attracts large crowds to his shrine.

And Dipalpur, forty kilometres further north, was once so great a centre of religion and learning it was rated second only to Multan. Today it's easy to miss it.

'Where are you from?'

The complete stranger's friendly, direct approach on the Shahrah-e-Quaid-e-Azam in Lahore was totally unexpected — but the experience was to prove typical. Most Pakistanis want to greet you, talk to you, and be friends. The young man made the point on the first day of a first ever visit to his country. A medical student at the University, it emerged later, he had simply tagged along as we walked toward the Anarkali bazaar, immediately launching conversation with his question.

Questions asked in such encounters can be politely ingenuous but at first disconcertingly direct and personal. 'Are you married?' . . . 'How many children?' . . . 'Why not?' are typically matter-of-fact inquiries. Indeed, they usually represent contact at a deeper, and some might say more genuine, level than talk about the weather.

Pakistanis are generally friendly people, deeply interested in others as people. And perhaps nowhere so spontaneously as in Lahore. But then — as those who know it will tell you — Lahore is different. Lahore is special.

For nearly a thousand years the city has inspired rhapsodies. It's beyond compare say many, superior to all other cities of the world. An ancient saying is typical — 'The man who hasn't seen Lahore hasn't lived' as are titles like 'The Queen of Cities', and 'Pearl of the Punjab'.

More popular with truck drivers — who perhaps hope the employers who send them there will get the message — is a less extravagant legend which advises: 'If you have money, go to Lahore; if you haven't, stay away.' Easily the most prosaic is what the quite unprosaic people who live there have said for centuries: 'Lahore is Lahore.'

It's known, above all, as the city of the Mughals. On that ground alone a cultural rival to Lahore in Pakistan is as unthinkable as a commercial rival to Karachi. No city has so many Mughal monuments of such excelling quality. The layout of the old city, the Fort, with all the evidence it contains of Mughal glory and splendour, the great mosques, the imperial mausolea, the incomparable gardens, are all the gifts of the Mughals or the work of Mughal inspiration.

But Lahore is at least 1,000 years older than the Mughals; and much good — as well as harm — has befallen the city since 1707 when the death of Aurangzeb, the last of the great Mughal emperors, deprived the Queen of Cities of its most jealous and powerful guardians.

Excavation has already proved there was a settlement at Lahore in the sixth century AD, though little is yet known of its first 400 years. Future research is expected to show that the city was founded long before that, probably before the Christian era. Inevitably Alexander the Great has been dragged in, either to found Lahore as Bucephalus in honour of the famous horse none but he could ride (that city, in fact, is almost certainly much further north-west, on the river Jhelum); or as a settlement for the serfs he left behind. There is no evidence for either claim.

Mohamed bin Qasim, who first brought Islam to the Indus Valley, never carried the faith as far north as Lahore. That distinction rests with Mahmud of Ghazni who invaded from the north-west in 1021. Lahore was then a stronghold of the Hindu Shahis, whose royal city was Kabul but whose power was under increasing challenge from the lords of nearby Ghazni.

Previous pages: Of red sandstone inlaid with white marble, Jahangir's magnificent mausoleum in Lahore has an arcaded gallery around its four sides. Richly-decorated corridors within lead to a central cenotaph carved from pure white marble.

Above: Classic Mughal miniature of Akbar the Great from a collection in Karachi Museum.

Opposite: Pastel yellow and rich green highlight the intricate and pleasing lines of Lahore's Dai Anga mosque, commissioned by Emperor Shah Jahan's wetnurse, after whom it is named.

Today's Lahore shows nothing of that pre-Mahmud Hindu past. Some claim, however, that the name Lahore is Hindu, and means Fort of Loh, son of Rama (the hero of the third century BC Sanskrit epic the *Ramayana*); and it's interesting that Lahore Fort — where archaeologists found evidence of sixth-century habitation — shows a temple dedicated to him. The nearby river Ravi is said to be named for a Hindu goddess. And there's a tradition that the old city's Bhatti Gate is named for Rajput families who emigrated in AD 145.

Whatever went before 1021, once Lahore settled down under Muslim rule it seems to have enjoyed a century and a half of prosperity that was like a Silver Age, prelude to the Golden Age of Mughal glory that would follow 500 years later. Scholars and poets, mystics and writers came to the city and settled there in such numbers that it became a leading cultural centre and, eventually, after Baghdad and Ghazni, the third city of Islam. In fact, trade flourished so well that for much of the time between 1059 and 1186 Lahore was effectively capital of the Ghazni dynasty.

Sadly, the silver was badly tarnished by the decline that quickly followed the seizure of power by a rival Afghan dynasty based on the city of Ghor. To them, Lahore was no more than an outpost for the defence of Delhi, the magnet which drew all invaders — both for its own wealth and because of the commanding position it held on the great trade routes to the east and west. As a mere outpost through the ensuing centuries, Lahore proved horribly vulnerable to visitation from those most terrible scourges of Asia — Genghis Khan and Tamurlane, and the fierce Khokkar tribesmen. There were times, it is said, when men had to be paid just to live in Lahore. In 1421 no living thing had its abode there 'except the owl of ill omen'.

Not surprising, then, that practically nothing remains of that Silver Age; 'practically', since the tomb of Malik Ayyaz, an early Ghazni governor of the city, who died in 1042, is still there in the old city. And — immensely important in Lahore today — the tomb of Data Ganj Bakhsh, 'the Saint who dispenses favours', the patron saint of Lahore and still the object of intense and widespread devotion.

A renowned scholar and mystic, Ali Mukdum Hajweri left Ghazni, his home town, to settle in Lahore in 1039. He spiced his constant preaching with such generosity, especially to the poor and needy, that in his lifetime he was nicknamed Data, 'the giver of gifts'. He died in 1072 and was buried close to a mosque he had had built.

Even today his cult, which never lapsed, flourishes with ancient fervour. Near the shrine a number of social services, including a medical dispensary and a public kitchen, have been provided, and a large new mosque has been built in recent years to accommodate the ever-growing numbers of worshippers who attend — nowadays in their thousands — the Thursday evening devotions on the eve of every week's Islamic Holy Day .

No visitor who has the time should miss the opportunity for a Thursday evening visit to this shrine. The weekly celebrations, characterised by religious music and gifts of food to the poor, generate an unforgettable atmosphere of warmth and humanity.

The Turkish-speaking Tiger, Babur (1483-1530), who founded the

Above: Classic Mughal miniature of the first of the Great Mughals, Babur.

Above: Centuries-old painting of the Chamra school shows a lady of the court being groomed.

Mughal dynasty and empire and so ushered in Lahore's Golden Age, came with a daunting pedigree.

On his father's side he was descended from Tamurlane, and on his mother's from Genghis Khan. The records of his prowess in battle show he was quite as fearless as his two forbidding forbears, but that he also possessed a refinement of mind they lacked.

Babur loved books, and while he could — and did — ransack the cities, towns, and villages he went to subdue, he was magnanimous in victory. The diaries he kept show him highly intellectual, a poet, and an aesthete with a passion for fountains and gardens as great as his love for battle.

This remarkable double edge to his talents and personality, the fierce and equal passions for creation and destruction, for physical violence and cultural refinement, represent perhaps the distinctive characteristic not just of Babur but of all the great Mughals descended from him. And Lahore, the Mughal city *par excellence*, wears the look of both characteristics.

The founder of the Mughal line built no monuments in Lahore. On the contrary, having been invited by a disgruntled rival governor of Lahore to come and take over the city, Babur arrived to find it armed to repel him. In anger, he overcame the defenders 'with great slaughter', plundered the city's wealth, and put its bazaars to the torch.

Ironically, because of the massive security which his empire provided, the first period of architecture which has any real significance in Lahore today is that of those mixed-up Lodhis who ruled immediately before him and invited him in to replace them.

The Niwin mosque in the old city is one example and a number of public buildings, including schools and a hospice which can still be seen, also date from their day.

Babur died in Agra in 1530 when he had established an empire in which Lahore was to be fortified, developed, and so embellished that for the Mughals it became second in importance only to Delhi.

The oldest surviving monument of that new empire, in fact, stands in Lahore. It was built by Babur's younger son, Kamran, who — already governor of Kabul and Kandahar while his father lived — seized Lahore in a bid for the succession against his older brother Humayun. He failed but Kamran nevertheless was allowed to rule over Lahore, which he immediately began to beautify with gardens and pavilions. One of these can still be seen, in ruins and now isolated by the fickle Ravi river which has carved courses on either side of it so that the only access is by boat.

Both brothers, Kamran and Humayun, ended their lives unhappily. Kamran plotted so persistently against Humayun that eventually even this untypical Mughal was stirred to action and had the treacherous prince's eyes put out and exiled him to a life of prayer in Makkah. After ten years on the Mughal throne he was deposed by the Afghan lord, Sher Shah Suri, who on his deathbed, lamented that he had not destroyed such a vulnerable pearl of a city as Lahore.

Humayun then spent fourteen years on the run, only to die — little more than a year after his Persian allies restored him to power — in a fall down the stairs of his Delhi observatory.

Like his father, Humayun bequeathed no buildings to Lahore. But,

Above: Intricate calligraphic inscriptions from the Qur'an in Lahore's Wazir Khan mosque, considered the finest of its kind in South Asia.

unlike Babur, he left a son whose acts eclipsed Babur's own. This was that Akbar who was born in the wilderness of Umarkot, in Sind. He was to establish Lahore on an eminence from which the worst of its subsequent misfortune failed to dislodge it. Appropriately his name, Akbar, means 'The Great'.

Still in his early teens when news of Humayun's death was received, Akbar was on his way to take up the governorship of Lahore under the guardianship of a general of renown, Bairam Khan. He was crowned forthwith, and the general was made his regent. At the age of eighteen Akbar assumed control of the Empire, and, even before 1584, when he made Lahore his capital city, he showed the city of his first command unique favour, and paid frequent personal visits.

Akbar's was no commonplace personality. Though short in stature he was immensely powerful. An uncompromising warrior, who strengthened and extended all the frontiers of his empire, he was ruthless and unschooled yet astonishingly liberal in his thinking, intellectually curious — especially in matters of religion — and endlessly innovative.

Above: Treasured Hindu depiction of Krishna in Lahore Museum.

The classic illustration of his ruthlessness is the story — dismissed nowadays as fable — of Anarkali, Pomegranate Bud. According to the legend, Akbar saw his son, Prince Salim (the future Jahangir), smiling at Anarkali — one of the beautiful young dancers in his harem — and suspected them of a secret affair and had the girl built into the city wall alive. Eventually, so the story goes, when Jahangir succeeded to the Mughal throne he commissioned the imposing monument that still bears the dancer's name at the place of her execution.

Inscriptions inside the tomb are now said to show that the monument was the burial-place of Jahangir's wife Sahib-i-Jamal, who died in 1599. Historians add that there never was a dancer called Anarkali, or even a woman of her ilk.

Some may think that they protest too much but, whatever its original purpose, 'Anarkali's tomb' has been put to a variety of uses since. During Sikh rule of the Punjab it was a residence. Under the British it was used as a Protestant church. And today it houses the Punjab Record Office and Archive Museum.

Akbar may truly be said to have founded modern Lahore. Before him,

Above: Classic Mughal miniature of Shah Jahan, the Architect King.

for all its importance, the city's walls were earthworks. Akbar levelled these, extended their base and replaced them with thirty-feet-high solid masonry walls. Access could be gained only through twelve gates. Half of these and most of his city wall were pulled down by the British, who also filled in the surrounding moat.

Why the British did this is unclear: whether in the interests of security or for the sake of public health. But six gates remain and they and the variety of their design suffice to show that Akbar's objective was twofold — to make Lahore both unusually attractive to live in and absolutely secure under attack.

Today the best view of the defences with which Akbar surrounded the city is probably on the east side of the Fort — where the great gate he built, the Akbari, and the walls on either side of it stand intact. Contemporaries able to compare this solid, no-nonsense, once-and-for-all masonry with the girdle of mud surmounted by wooden platforms it replaced must have been deeply impressed with Akbar's high ambitions for the Queen of Cities.

The oldest surviving dated mosque in Lahore stands near this Akbari (also known as the Masti) Gate. Constructed on the orders of Akbar's wife, Maryam Zamani — the mother of Jahangir — this lovely little building is remarkable for its dome and for the frescos that delicately intertwine floral and geometric designs with Qur'anic inscriptions in Naskh characters. These are considered the finest Mughal frescos anywhere. Under the Sikhs the building was used as a powder magazine. It was restored to the Muslims in 1850.

Inside the Fort the finest structures are the work of Akbar's grandson, Shah Jahan. But almost certainly Akbar is responsible for the fine central Hall of Public and Private Audience, the *Daulat Khan-i-Khas-o-Aam.* Although defaced, enough of its internal decor remains, including gold, to give an idea of the original splendour. The many little galleries and reception rooms, decorated with frescos and floral motifs in stucco, create an atmosphere of behind-the-scenes intimacy that warms the otherwise impersonal solemnity that surrounded the Emperor and his successors on their way out to the *Jharoka,* or Balcony of State.

This small, superbly-open yet aloof white marble platform on brackets of red sandstone is where Akbar presented himself to be adored by his people as a ray of the sun he worshipped.

It was sight of this unexpected procedure that dashed the hopes of the Goan Jesuits who had been so encouraged by the courtesy Akbar showed them that they had begun to entertain ideas of his eventual conversion to Christianity.

Ambassadors, returning envoys, visitors, and other supplicants waited here for audience, and from this vantage point Akbar and the other great Mughals daily reviewed the displays of pomp and power that dazzled Europeans with their grandeur and magnificence.

Akbar was fascinated by almost everything. His curiosity was insatiable. During his reign meetings were held on the evening of every Sabbath to discuss 'profound points of science, the subtleties of revelation, the curiosities of history and the wonders of Nature'. Indeed, often whole nights were dedicated to these discussions, the Emperor in attendance throughout. Sometimes passions got out of hand. An eminent mullah who insulted the Prophet was tied to the foot of an elephant and dragged through the streets of Lahore till he was dead. Even that wasn't enough.

As soon as Akbar left the city to campaign in Kashmir, despite a guard over the burial place the mangled remains were disinterred and burned.

Akbar finally elaborated his own Universal Religion, with elements drawn from such diverse sources as Persian astrology, pantheism, and Christianity. But he always denied he was a heretic.

Above the Hall of Public and Private Audience, the flat roof with the Mughal watchtower offers a superb view of the area known as Jahangir's quadrangle which, despite its name, was laid out by Akbar. Perhaps it was here that one of the Emperor's most intriguing and fascinating projects was accomplished.

Details are lost, but in a typical exercise of his ever-active and curious mind, Akbar had a water tank built in the fort so designed that somehow its floor gave onto a perfectly dry and beautifully-furnished and equipped dining room.

Outside the Fort, too, Akbar built hospices for poor Hindus as well as for poor Muslims. (Part of this last, the Khyrpura, remains near Daranagar on the road to Mian Mir). It is recorded that the Hindu hospice also sheltered 'Jews and fire-worshippers' and that when Jogis flocked to the site for help Akbar had a separate Jogipura built for them.

Other institutions of the period were a royal Mint, a carpet factory, and gardens — for which Akbar invited Persian experts to come and cultivate the grape and the melon.

Akbar encouraged the most distinguished scholars, writers, poets, musicians, and thinkers of the day to settle in Lahore, ordered histories written, epics translated, and illustrations made. His Prime Minister, Abu-al-Fazal, a scholar whose writings won universal admiration as 'model and despair of the age', described Lahore in 1557 as 'the resort of all nations and a centre of extensive commerce. In the shortest time great armies can be collected there and ammunitions of war in any quantity can be procured for the use of troops'.

Akbar launched many of his great military campaigns from Lahore, including those against Afghanistan, Swat, and Bajaur. And out of Lahore, doubtless cause for particular satisfaction, he brought Thatta and the Sind, where he was born, into the Empire.

Akbar ruled for half a century and made Lahore his capital for the most brilliant fourteen years of his reign — 1584-1598. His three great successors, too, made much of Lahore.

His son, Prince Salim, was especially surprising. His liking for alcohol and drugs made Akbar think long and hard before, on his deathbed, naming him his successor. Salim, who had more than once angered his father by trying to anticipate this event, named himself Jahangir — Conqueror of the World — and quickly demonstrated the Mughal ruthlessness that was in him.

His older son, Khusrow, encouraged by disaffected courtiers, decided to rebel, and marched on Lahore to secure a base for attacks on Delhi and Agra. He got no further than the Lahore city gates. Forces loyal to Jahangir routed his army and the hapless Khusrow was brought before his father in a garden just outside Lahore. Jahangir spared his son's life,

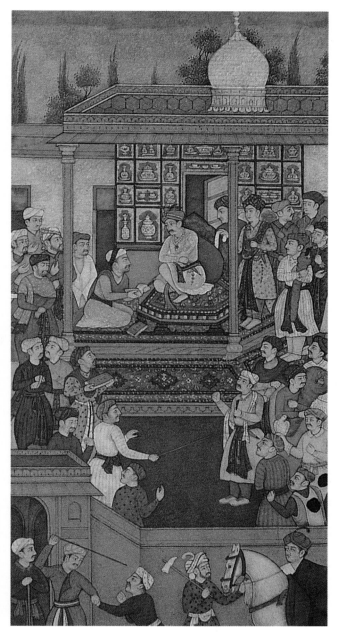

Above: Court of the Great Mughals, a period depiction now in the Faqir Khana family museum.

but had 700 of his captured followers impaled alive on an avenue of sharp stakes leading into Lahore. Khusrow, on an elephant, was then conducted through the grisly lines by a mace-bearer who called out for him to receive the greetings of his followers.

At the same time, Jahangir possessed an extraordinarily cultivated mind and showed himself capable of strict self-discipline, bravery in battle, and justice in judgement. He was well-read and himself a good writer.

Like his father he was liberal and tolerant in matters of religion. He demonstrated a special reverence for Muslim holy men, and when in Agra even sent for Mian Mir, known as 'the saint of Lahore', to get his advice.

'Truly', Jahangir wrote after this meeting, 'he is the beloved of God. In sanctity and purity of heart he has no equal in this age.'

The diary also records a meeting with Maulana Mohamed Amin, also of Lahore. 'Notwithstanding his worldly connections he is distinguished by independence of character and contentment, and command over his spirit.'

Remarkable thoughts from a man who broke a rebellion on gory stakes and viewed the scene from the tower where his father used to watch elephant fights.

Both inside and outside Lahore Jahangir commissioned and inspired much building. At Sheikhupura, thirty-one kilometres north-west of Lahore, he laid out one of the most charming beauty spots of the region. Passionately fond of hunting on this ground, then called Jahangirabad, he kept there a favourite antelope called Mans Raj. When the animal died he raised a life-size stone statue over the grave as a monument and thenceforth banned deer-hunting within the park. Later, he had the huge water tank and nearby tower built. His own son, Shah Jahan, changed them to meet his own even more exacting standards of design. The park remains an attractive and much-favoured spot for outings from Lahore.

Of Jahangir's many buildings in and immediately around the city, the most impressive are the quandrangle in the fort which bears his name and the Fort's famous Picture Wall — finished by his son, Shah Jahan. Jahangir's quadrangle — started by Akbar — is one of the Fort's most enchanting areas. Most of it is garden, laid out in geometric beds about a central tank containing more than thirty fountains. In the east and west, a series of porticoed lodges in red sandstone, with richly carved columns and brackets engagingly sculpted in the forms of elephants, lions, and other animals, show how Akbar and Jahangir were influenced by Hindu tradition in art. The south side of the quadrangle is taken up by Akbar's Halls of Audience, the north by Jahangir's sleeping chambers, now used as a museum.

In its prime the Fort's famous Picture Wall must have been a breathtaking sight. It covered 745 square metres of the Fort's north-western corner with glazed tiles depicting an enormous range of subjects in unsurpassed brilliance of colour. Geometric designs, animals, and people all feature in compositions that show the sports and other amusements that entertained Mughal emperors, as well as some of their more serious preoccupations — polo, wrestling, hunting, elephant and bull and gladiator fights, music, mythology, and religion.

Above: Multi-coloured flowers of inlaid stone at the base of one of the Shish Mahal's supporting columns.

Above: Detail from Lahore Fort's famous Picture Wall.

Time has taken its toll of this superb achievement, not least in removing the Ravi river to a different bed. When the Picture Wall was built the river flowed under it. Originally, therefore, the superb effect of the faience mosaics was duplicated — each of the bold-coloured horses and elephants, dragons, courtiers and warriors on the wall fighting and chasing and playing and parrying a second time in the mirror images shimmering in the sun-bright water below. Happily, enough remains to charge the imagination and inspire wonder still.

Today, the river Ravi flows four or five kilometres north of the old city wall. On its other side, at Shah Dara, stands one of Lahore's greatest monuments — Jahangir's mausoleum. It is the largest work in a complex of grandeur that introduces the visitor to one of the most dazzling personalities in the rich Mughal gallery — a woman who loved life and Lahore, Jahangir's Empress, Nur Jahan. She owned the park, Dilkusha, in which her husband's body lies, but it's not clear whether his superb mausoleum is her work or Shah Jahan's.

Nur Jahan was the daughter of a Persian nobleman forced to flee his own country whose ability quickly took him to the post of Prime Minister under Jahangir.

Jahangir married Nur Jahan, who was famous for beauty and brains, in 1611. Their relationship reads like a mix of German and Italian romantic opera lightened here and there with a dash of Gilbert and Sullivan, but despite periods of hypertense alienation it was his will that he should be buried in her garden, and hers that his final wish should be granted.

The mausoleum is a huge, square, arcaded building in red sandstone with white marble inlay. The corners are elegantly crowned with minarets of white marble. Richly decorated corridors lead from each side to the central cenotaph in white marble on a *pietra dura* inlaid platform. The tomb's calligraphy is especially notable. The sides list the ninety-nine names of Allah. At the head is the *Kalima* in Arabic; at the foot, the name and dates of the Emperor.

The mausoleum suffered serious damage during Sikh rule. Its restoration was begun by the British in 1889. In its garden setting, surrounded by trees, pools, and fountains it speaks eloquently of the marvellous confidence and refinement that lived side-by-side with incredible cruelty in the Jekyll and Hyde minds of the Mughals.

To reach Jahangir's mausoleum, you must pass through the confusingly named Akbari Serai, the work of Jahangir's younger son, Shah Jahan, builder of the Taj Mahal in Agra, and universally acclaimed greatest of all the Mughal builders. His serai, next to the Dilkusha, exemplifies perfectly the skill he had in bringing huge expanse into a unity the mind can enjoy.

The idea was to build a resting place for travellers, and this was provided by means of four massive walls which vault no fewer than 180 porchlike arches where travellers could cook, relax, and sleep secure.

The corners accommodate more elaborate 'burjs' or pavilions. The British used the serai as a railway goods depot, but it's hard to believe. A spacious garden, with trees, fills the area between the serai walls and makes one think that western camping grounds, for all their mod-con facilities, have a long way to go yet.

Before leaving this corner of Lahore two other monuments should be remarked. Nur Jahan had a brother called Asaf Khan. His daughter was the Mumtaz Mahal whom Shah Jahan married, and whose death in childbirth inspired him to build, as her monument, what many count the most beautiful building of all time, the Taj Mahal.

Asaf Khan is buried close to the Lahore serai — in a dilapidated monument which is, in some ways, the more impressive for its sorry condition.

Stripped of its marble ornamentation during the nineteenth century, a bare-bones building remains to confront the visitor today. Without any gleam or sparkle, the emphatic simplicity of the dome on its arcaded, octagonal base is an architect's model of the way the Mughals achieved their particular marriage of weightiness and acceptability. For all their uncompromising, almost ruthless power, Mughal buildings do not crush or overwhelm the viewer the way much twentieth-century western architecture does. It can always be seen as a powerful, but pleasing, whole.

Nur Jahan herself was buried only one and a half kilometres away. For

Above: Lahore mausoleum of Nur Jahan, wife of the Mughal Emperor Jahangir, 'Conqueror of the World', who virtually ruled the empire during her husband's final years.

Overleaf: Lahore Fort's famous Shish Mahal — 'Hall of Mirrors' — in Shah Jahan's palace takes its name from the leaded glass inlaid in the walls and ceiling. The screen beyond the central arch is of carved marble.

Above: Relieved by intricately fine stone inlay, Lahore Fort's Naulakha, in pure white marble, was said to be a favourite pavilion for the women of Shah Jahan's court.

her beauty, brilliance, and power — she virtually ruled the Empire in Jahangir's last years — her many enemies followed her, even to the grave it seems. Her mausoleum was robbed of all decoration during Sikh rule; even her cenotaph and that of the daughter buried with her were violated.

A considerable amount of restoration has been completed and a garden of roses, her favourite flower, planted round the mausoleum. It deserves a visit; but there is something inescapably sad about what happened to the grave of a woman who loved Lahore so much that she lived her last, eighteen widowed years there and uttered that haunting, mysterious farewell:

'I have purchased Lahore with my life. By giving my life for Lahore, actually I have purchased another Paradise.'

Shah Jahan, who was born in Lahore in 1592, endowed the city of his birth with by far the largest number of its Mughal buildings — many of its finest among them. But if he is architecturally the most prolific and successful of the dynasty he showed an even darker side to his cruelty than earlier Mughals.

Opposite: Daulat Khana pavilion — the Deer Tower — at Sheikhupura, formerly Jahangirabad, was started by Jahangir in honour of his favourite antelope and completed by his son, Shah Jahan.

It had long been rumoured that he was behind the mysterious 1621 murder of his older brother Khusrow. And on his accession to the throne in 1628 he proved that he was indeed capable of such a crime. He celebrated his coronation with an orgy of domestic blood-letting — executing, as 'rivals' to his throne, all his male relatives including a nephew still a child, who had been used by his own partisans to complicate the claim of a more plausible contender.

Murder of immediate family was an excess that previous Mughals had denied themselves, and Shah Jahan lived to regret the precedent. His son, Aurangzeb, had all his brothers killed.

The greatest concentration of Shah Jahan's building works in Lahore is in the Fort. Its most spectacular area — the north-west corner, with the Picture Wall (which he completed) on the external face — is all his.

Behind the Picture Wall, he built a grand entrance gate, brightly decorated with mosaics, giving onto a huge fifty-eight-step stairway, seven metres broad and sixty-five metres long, to accommodate elephants carrying members of the royal family and of the harem. From niches and galleries built into the stairway wall, heralds proclaimed arrivals and departures.

This stairway led directly to the Shah Burj or Royal Palace, built originally about a single courtyard, but divided, during Sikh rule, with a wall. Today's visitor sees first the Athdara built by the Sikhs, in which their most successful ruler, Ranjit Singh, dispensed justice. Its frescos show Krishna celebrating the Spring Festival.

In the second half of the courtyard is the quadrangular Burj itself, one of the most profusely-decorated monuments of the entire Mughal period, and used by the Emperor as his residence when in Lahore. The 1845 Treaty of Lahore, which handed the Punjab to Britain and so ended Sikh rule in Lahore, was signed here.

This is also, according to some authorities, where the largest of the British Crown Jewels — the Koh-i-Noor diamond, estimated at over 229 carats — was handed over to the British. The central room, richly-studded with mirrors and therefore named the Shish Mahal, Palace of Mirrors, is carried on superbly-worked double columns, across five, handsomely-scalloped arches. The back wall is embellished with marble screening of extraordinary beauty, carved with geometrical and floral designs.

The floor demands attention. A variety of marbles makes the setting for the central pool basin, which is designed to give an impression of waves.

The courtyard is finished with what many consider the most charming little building in the Fort: the Bungla, or Naulakha. The first name refers to the Bengali, downward-curving style of the roof. This delicate, marble pavilion is said to have been a favourite with the women of the harem for the view its marble screening gave them, themselves unseen, of the city below.

'Naulakha', nine lakhs, refers to the cost of this little edifice. It was an enormous sum, largely explained by the intricacy of decoration. In the portico, more than 100 semi-precious stones can be counted in the composition of a single flower.

Sketch it and soon a group of wondering, dark-eyed children will form to watch. 'You like this place, I can see,' their father informs you. 'It is very historical. Where are you from . . . ?' The fort attracts many Pakistani visitors — the men often bearded or moustached and tending to seriousness, the girls and women usually in groups, all smiles and laughter, their bright-coloured garb and bearing bringing welcome life and grace to the garden paths and monuments they visit.

Adjacent to Jahangir's, Shah Jahan has his quadrangle. The contrast is fascinating. The father's, with its warm red sandstone and the animal carvings, glows with the warmth and simplicity of a child; the son's, classically cool in marble, was conjured by genius.

On the north side, the Hall of Private Audience (*Diwan-i-Khas*) is an arched pavilion all in white except for the *pietra dura* embellishment of the parapet and the floor of multi-coloured marble. A fountain with more *pietra dura* inlay plays artlessly in the centre. Everything's marble, even the ceiling. The latticed, marble screens on the north side are of superb craftsmanship. The Emperor's sleeping quarters (*Khawabgah*) opposite, and Royal Bath (*Hamman*) on the west side, have both lost much of their original marble, and Sikh frescos and tracery conceal the original decoration.

The summer pavilion (*Lal Burj*) in the north-west corner was added to by the Sikhs (the top third), and the British used it as a bar; but the gilded honeycomb cornice that remains is enough to show how lavish the decoration once was. The middle storey is surrounded by a duct carrying water from a central fountain to cool the air.

The famous Pearl Mosque (*Moti Masjid*), small yet regal in the pure marble for which it is named, stands off a quiet garden: a young queen, with the secret of eternal youth.

Possibly the most evocative area of the Fort is the Hall of Public Audience (*Diwan-i-Aam*) built by Shah Jahan to add yet more splendour to the Emperor's daily public appearances. Previously, the dignitaries assembled under the *Jharoka* to be received by the Emperor were protected from the weather by awnings. Shah Jahan commissioned the building of a large open hall — fifty-six metres long and eighteen broad — standing on a larger platform edged by a red sandstone railing to match the forty pillars, eleven metres high, that carry the arches bearing the roof. A second railing in white marble has been lost. Surrounding the huge platform were vaulted apartments, with gateways in the middle of the south, west, and east sides (the apartments have since given way to open gardens).

In this airy arcade, built about the *Jharoka*, little imagination is needed to see and hear the multi-coloured and caparisoned ranks of Mughal nobility and their retainers, the ambassadors, generals, and returning State envoys, already assembled — to each his place appointed according to the physical demarcation of strict imperial protocol and its fussing ministers, some with abounding confidence, others anxious, excited, awed, others perhaps full of fears — as they wait for the entry of the Emperor, this descendant of Babur, of Tamurlane and of Ghengis Khan, this great, terrible Mughal Lord of Hindustan, the Absolute ruler, the Shah-in-Shah, the King of Kings.

The deference due to the Mughals, and its practical expression, was obviously beyond question. 'On the 9th,' records a visitor to Lahore,

Opposite: High above Akbar the Great's 'Lahori Gate', at centre, a modern mosque, right, stands guard over the chaotic traffic of downtown Lahore.

'Wazir Khan presented his Majesty with jewels, gold and silver utensils, rich stuffs, carpets, horses and camels valued at four lakhs of rupees, which he had collected during the period of his vice-royalty in the Punjab. The same day Said Khan, Subedar of Kabul, having had the honour of an audience, presented his Majesty with 1,000 ashrafis, 100 horses and 100 camels. Kalich Khan, governor of Multan, made a present of 18 horses of Irak, together with curiosities of Persia. . . . The whole of the presents amounted to ten lakhs of rupees.'

Next time Shah Jahan visited Lahore, the same Wazir Khan — a man who obviously had his priorities right — presented him with a travelling throne of gold, fifty horses from Irak, and other 'curiosities' valued at two lakhs.

But the Mughals, too, well knew the value of munificence. In 1631, the court was again in session in Lahore when the governor of Kandahar — a Persian possession for the last ten years — arrived and surrendered the keys of his city to Shah Jahan. Not surprisingly, the Mughal received governor Ali Mardan Khan very kindly indeed and made him an Amir of the first rank. 'The Khan, having paid his obeisance, offered his majesty a gift of 1,000 gold pieces, and was honoured with silk and embroidered clothes, a jewelled turban with aigrette, a jewelled dagger, shield and sword.'

The new Amir was also allowed 6,000 staff and given two horses with embroidered saddles and four elephants with silver housings. The enormous expense of the ex-Governor's trip from Kandahar was also recognised — all paid by the State treasury. And 'as he had come from a fertile and cool country the Emperor was pleased to appoint him to the governorship of Kashmir'. All in all, one cannot help reflecting, a good day's work for a governor who had seen all he wanted to of Kandahar.

At this time, Lahore was at the height of its splendour. 'Besides the countless military retainers of the Emperor, the picturesque cavalcades of the Princes Royal and the attendants of the numerous nobles and grandees of State, the sight of the Governors and Viceroys of provinces from the Narbada and Tapti to the confines of Kandahar and Ghazni, and their vast hosts of followers who came here to pay their homage to the King of Kings, afforded a most imposing and gorgeous spectacle. Here came also the envoys of foreign nations, the bearers of friendly letters to the Emperor, or of the curiosities of their respective countries to present to him. . . .'

The quondam governor of Kandahar rose rapidly. Later that same year he was appointed Viceroy of Lahore and Kashmir with a rank of 7,000 staff and 7,000 horses. In return, he was permitted to entertain the Emperor with a Persian-style firework show in the Fort. The Emperor loved it and gave the poor 10,000 rupees.

Liberality was accounted virtue among the Mughals. 'On the 15th his majesty visited the mausoleum of Jahangir and distributed 10,000 rupees to the poor, while 5,000 rupees were distributed to the princes who accompanied him. His majesty, who entertained much respect for the fakirs, paid a visit to the saint, Mian Mir. His majesty, knowing that he cared not for worldly wealth, presented him with a rosary and a turban of white cloth and received his blessing.'

In 1634 when heavy rains and flooding ruined the harvest, thousands

Above: Since the days of the Great Mughals who endowed the city with its first pleasure parks, Lahore has been known as the 'City of Gardens'. The tradition is maintained with such pleasant examples of landscaping as the post-Independence Gulshan-i-Iqbal gardens.

of peasants approached the *Jharoka* for help. 'The Emperor was pleased to grant a lakh of rupees for their relief, and it was ordered that as long as they stayed in the capital, food should be distributed to them daily.' Kashmir suffered, too, and 50,000 rupees were sent for the relief of famine victims there.

Five years later the Ali Mardan Khan who handed over Kandahar instigated what was to become one of Shah Jahan's best-loved creations — the Shalamar Gardens. The Persian's contribution was to suggest that Lahore would benefit greatly if a canal were built from Rajpur to bring Ravi river water to the city.

The 160-kilometre-long Royal Canal took two years to build, and when it was completed the Emperor charged another nobleman, Khalilullah Khan, with the task of finding a suitable site for a royal pleasure garden of classical Mughal design, fed by the waters of the Royal Canal. On 31 October, 1642, eighteen months after the foundations were laid, Shah Jahan went in state to visit the newly-completed Shalamar Gardens.

'A garden,' wrote Babur, 'is the purest of human pleasures.' Compared with the endless aridity and cruel heat of Hindustan, his

Opposite: Now an improbable twentieth-century playground for citizens of Lahore, the incomparable Shalamar Gardens of Shah Jahan were commissioned as a royal pleasure garden.

ancestral, central Asian home was cool, with abundant, clean spring waters bringing constant refreshment to body and soul.

Gardens were his and his followers' answer to the shortcomings of the subcontinent. Their mathematical order favoured repose, while shade and plentiful water supplied the sorely-missed cool, and the feeling of physical ease.

Hence the typical Mughal garden — walled, with terraces and the shade of flower and fruit trees, walks and trees and shrubs geometrically ordered, and everywhere the air cooled by fountains and pools of flowing water.

Such is the refreshment awaiting today's visitor, six kilometres or so north of the city on the Great Trunk road. Nowadays you enter at the highest of the three terrace levels, but originally entrance was from the bottom, so that only one level was visible until you climbed up and 'discovered' the second and, subsequently, what is today the first.

First and third terraces are gigantic squares, each divided into quarters by water channels, decorated with red sandstone and marble fountains, running north-south and east-west. There are larger pools with more fountains where the channels intersect. Water, running down the six-metre-wide central canals of the top and bottom terraces, and filling the central pool of the middle level, ties the whole design together.

The heart of the garden is the central terrace, an oblong as wide as the other terraces, but only seventy-eight metres long. It is in three sections: the middle one the great, sixty-metre-wide pool with over 100 fountains, four pavilions, and the Great Cascade, one of the Gardens' loveliest features. A great white marble wedge, the cascade's sculpted surface carries the water of the upper terrace down into the central tank in a way that contrives the effect of brilliantly-cascading diamonds. At its foot stands the Emperor's marble throne.

From the enchanting pavilions at the side you can walk a causeway to the marble-fenced platform in the middle of the pool specifically designed, one recognises instinctively, for evening relaxation with friends under the moon, surrounded by the playing fountains — and not a combustion engine or a jet in the whole wide world to disturb the peace.

The Shalamar Gardens had many other amenities — sleeping quarters and pavilions, public and private audience halls, a bath house, gates, towers. It was all badly ravaged when Mughal power declined, but since then, to a great extent, restored.

As always happened, the royal building example was followed by leading ministers and those who wanted to catch the Emperor's eye. The supreme example is the mosque built by Governor Wazir Khan, generally considered the finest mosque of any age in south Asia. The outer face of the exterior is resplendent with mosaics, and frescos adorn the inside of the entrance bays. Powerful Persian influence is evident in the floral, geometric, and calligraphic decoration. This influence is traced back to Humayun, Shah Jahan's grandfather, who was restored to his throne largely through Persian aid.

Shah Jahan himself used Persian masters, inviting them to come and train his artists and craftsmen and supervise their work. All over Lahore, the many buildings commissioned during his reign gave employment to

Opposite: Shah Jahan's Shalamar Gardens have defied centuries of abuse and plunder to remain part of Lahore's incomparable heritage.

hundreds of painters, masons, workers in stone inlay, mosaics, and glass. All the rooms of the Fort were carpeted with the products of the emperor's Lahore Carpet Factory, beside which the finest from Persia were said to look like rough canvas.

In 1657, Shah Jahan was deposed, and held captive in Agra by his third son, Aurangzeb, for the rest of his days. Immensely talented, like his forbears, Aurangzeb also had his full share of the cruelty that was in them, pursuing his older brother, Dara Shikoh, the heir apparent and darling of Lahore, to his death, and grievously antagonising the majority Hindu population by enforcing Sharia law to the letter with great severity. There was rebellion in Delhi, but as long as Aurangzeb lived Lahore was virtually exempt from these troubles.

The outstanding mark of favour Aurangzeb showed the city is the building which, more than any other, has come to symbolise Mughal Lahore, the Badshahi Mosque. The last of the Great Mughals ordered its construction during a visit to the city in 1662. He told the congregation at a Friday Prayer meeting in a mosque that occupied the site previously that they must for ever assemble to pray on that spot.

Modelled on the Jamia mosques of Delhi and Agra, the Badshahi, with an official capacity of 60,000 worshippers, is more massive than either of its predecessors.

Constructed entirely of brick, dressed with red limestone, and ornamented with white marble domes, carvings, mosaics and frescos, the mosque occupies a 170-metre square atop a platform mounted via twenty-two steep steps. This main, eastern entry is pure Mughal and quite superb, from the elegant, cusped central arch to the white marble caps on the red sandstone, corner turrets.

The corners of the mosque are finished the same way, but much bolder, with fifty-three-metre-high minarets (Sher Singh, one of Ranjit Singh's sons, used them as cannon positions for shelling the Fort in 1841).

Inside the mosque, facing the entrance, the Prayer Hall on its twenty-five by eighty-two metre platform is relatively small; but its red sandstone crenellated walls, minareted corner towers, and massive interior arches are all perfectly proportioned to carry effortlessly the spectacular white domes. The *mirhab* and its corner stones are faced in marble.

Arcades around the vast court are a rebuilding. Originally the walls housed study rooms, but in 1856 the British demolished them — apparently for security reasons.

Immediately opposite the eastern entrance to the Badshahi mosque stands Aurangzeb's other great contribution to Lahore's store of Mughal architecture, the realigned wall of the Fort and its dominant feature, the Alamgiri gate. Aurangzeb ordered them rebuilt to make the Fort wall parallel with the east front of his new mosque.

The enormous gate — named from one of the emperor's titles, 'Conqueror of the Universe' — is flanked by semi-circular, fluted bastions topped with domed turrets. It wears the look of military intransigence associated with Aurangzeb and recalls the remark of an opponent: 'To fight Aurangzeb is to fight one's own fate.'

The last of the Great Mughals reigned longer than any of his

predecessors and when he died in the Deccan in 1707 — still fighting to extend his power to the south — no part of the empire had greater cause for lament than Lahore. Aurangzeb's successors, men without vision, neglected the Queen of Cities, the Pearl of the Punjab, to their own and their empire's inestimable loss.

Bereft of royal patronage the city once again fell prey to the ravages, plunder, and destruction it had known before Babur. Except that now the city's strength was in brick, stone, and marble, not earth; and enormous wealth had accumulated in the suburbs.

Eighteenth-century Lahore was a prize for new rulers to exploit rather than just a pearl to plunder. First the Sikhs, from 1768 to 1849, and then the British, until Independence, ran the city and did what they pleased with its monuments and treasures. Both behaved like iconoclasts in this stronghold of Mughal glory. But both also made positive contributions to the architectural riches of today's city.

Among the Sikhs one name is outstanding. Ranjit Singh ruled for forty years from 1799. He was illiterate but endowed with a lively mind, and he regularly consulted both Muslim and Hindu counsellors. When he died, the *samadhi* built for his ashes gave Lahore one of its most eye-catching monuments: bubbling with minarets in vivid contrast to the classic Mughal refinement of the Badshahi mosque next to it. Together with the gilded, fluted dome of the adjacent tomb of guru Arjan Dev, the *samadhi* is counted among the best Sikh monuments in Lahore.

Apart from the mighty fortification wall they erected north of the Fort, the most distinctive of the other Sikh buildings are the numerous mansions (*havelis*) like that of Jamadar Kushal Singh near the Fort, and those of Kallu Bai Ahluwalia, inside the Yakki gate, and Dhayan Singh, in the Hira Mandi district. Many of these are now used as Government offices. The Sikhs also created many gardens (*baghs*) but with rare exceptions these are now lost.

The British who, we have already seen, pulled down Lahore's Mughal walls, also sacrificed vast old areas of the city — complete with ancient mosques and mausolea, bazaars, and city residences — to the railway's immense appetite for land. Lahore always was (as it remains) pivotal in the country's railway system. But the benefits this has brought, incalculable though they may be, hardly justify the destruction (also incalculable) that went before them in Lahore.

Happily, in Lord Curzon the British appointed a Viceroy who stopped the destruction and did what he could to reverse the ravages by restoring the Fort, the Shalamar Gardens, Jahangir's mausoleum, and many others. He also established a government department dedicated to the preservation of ancient monuments.

With the improbable, but marvellously successful, hybrid of styles now called 'Mughal-Victorian' the British had already started to make their own, positive contribution to Lahore's rich architectural legacy. The many notable examples include the High Court, the (old) Punjab University, the Provincial Assembly, the General Post Office, the Town Hall, and the Free Masonic Lodge — happily preserved as a Museum of Punjab Arts and Crafts. In the same style are most of the fine schools and colleges which form the basis of Lahore's dominance, even today, in the realm of education: Government College, Foreman Christian College,

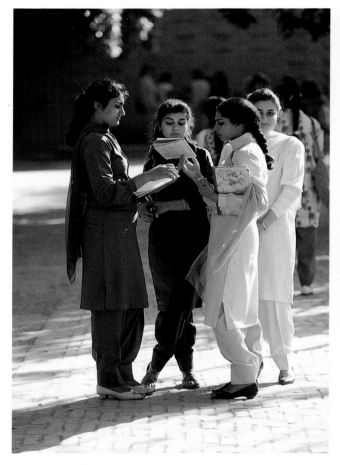

Above: Student break between classes at Lahore's Kinnaird College.

Opposite: Cast in Lahore in 1757, 'Zamzama', now standing outside Lahore Museum, was made famous by Nobel laureate Rudyard Kipling whose father, Lockwood, was the Museum's first curator. For the Sikhs who conquered Punjab it became a talisman. They said of it, 'Whoever holds Zamzama, holds Punjab'.

Islamia College, the Kinnaird College for Women, and Aitcheson (Chiefs) — the most expensive in the country.

Lahore Museum, in red sandstone behind its white marble entrance, is especially important. It is Pakistan's finest museum and has an outstanding collection of coins, paintings and sculptures. The 50,000 coins go back to the sixth century BC and include the best Indo-Greek examples anywhere on the subcontinent. The 2,000 paintings include the earliest and best-known collection of Punjab Hill Schools works, and the sculptures are dominated by the unique Fasting Buddha and other masterpieces from Gandhara. The exotic blend of Greek and Buddhist traditions they represent can be admired in many exhibits in this marvellous collection.

A relic of one of Lahore's many vagrant rulers stands in the middle of the road outside the museum. *Zamzama*, the gun, was made for a minister of the Afghan, Ahmad Shah Durrani, who used Lahore as a base for attacks on Delhi in the nineteenth century. The gun eventually passed into the possession of Ranjit Singh. Rudyard Kipling, whose father was curator of Lahore Museum, popularised it as 'Kim's Gun'.

In no sense Mughal, but classically-elegant, the Lawrence Montgomery Hall commemorates Sir John Lawrence, Chief Commissioner for the Punjab (1858-9) and the first Lieutenant-Governor, Sir Robert Montgomery (1859-63). Today it is a library dedicated to the memory of Quaid-i-Azam.

The most eloquent, early protagonist of the national independence which Pakistan acquired under the Quaid's leadership was the philosopher and scholar poet, Allama Muhammad Iqbal. He was born in Sialkot, ninety-six kilometres to the north, but lived most of his life in Lahore where he is buried close to the main entrance to the Badshahi mosque, a place that reflects his eminent contribution to the creation of Pakistan.

Iqbal told the All-India Muslim League in 1930 that for healthy development of Islam in south Asia, a separate Muslim state was essential. Two years after Iqbal's death, on 23 March 1940, the League met in Lahore and formulated the now famous 'Pakistan Demand' which seven years later, under Quaid-i-Azam's brilliant leadership, led to the country's birth. That 'Pakistan Demand' is commemorated in Iqbal Park by the most outstanding of Lahore's modern monuments — the Minar-i-Pakistan. And on 14 August, 1947, when the independent Republic came into being as a Federation, Lahore carried the flag of the capital of West Pakistan.

By an interesting historical coincidence the population of Lahore in 1947 when Pakistan achieved Independence was the same as it was when Akbar took the city's development in hand in the sixteenth century — half a million. Despite, or perhaps rather because of, the enormous problems the new country has faced since 1947 — including long periods of martial law, three major wars with its eastern neighbour, the loss of its eastern province (now Bangladesh) and, in the 1980s, the influx of an

Above: The room in Lahore where Allama Mohamed Iqbal, the poet and philosopher who first gave vision to the shape of Pakistan, died, is now a national monument and library.

Above: Grecian facade of Lahore's Quaid-i-Azam Library built more than a century ago as a memorial to two of Queen Victoria's senior servants on the subcontinent, Sir John Lawrence, Commissioner of Punjab 1858-59, and Sir Robert Montgomery, Lieutenant-Governor from 1859 to 1863.

Opposite: Allama Mohamed Iqbal was the first to promote the idea of a sovereign independent state for the subcontinent's Muslims.

estimated three million refugees from Afghanistan — Lahore's population has mushroomed to four million. A fifth could well be added before the end of the century.

Physically the city has grown so much that the ancient centre on which it is all based now appears astonishingly small: like the heart in the human body. Above all, the growth is to the south, where government-sponsored housing schemes and shopping centres, university and research establishments, industrial engineering plants and other facilities are creating, in effect, a new Lahore.

Yet the city retains its ancient charm. Already on the way in from the airport the visitor who arrives by air is impressed with Lahore's fine tree-lined boulevards, the lawns, flower-beds and gardens which have been a feature of the city for centuries.

Besides its architecture the city is famed too for its many popular festivals — notably the Fair of Lamps — while the Horse and Cattle Show in spring is at once a showcase for the country's livestock and a national play centre, with displays of Pakistan's innumerable and colourful folk-dances and other traditional entertainments.

Probably it is this felt continuity with the city's rich past that, in its lively and ever-expanding present, makes a visit to Lahore a different, quite special experience.

Not far from Lahore, paths and roads wind tortured ways around and between freak-shaped wedges of ore-filled rock. Waterways wander to where the mud bed of an ancient river, wide as the sea's when the tide is out, veers to the east, and sharp ravines score the dark, rugged plateau behind. Here the highest mountains on earth, that wall off Pakistan's north, finally step down over the last, low, tormented spread of the Salt Range onto the almost sea-level Punjab Plain.

Invaders from the north and north-west came this way to plunder

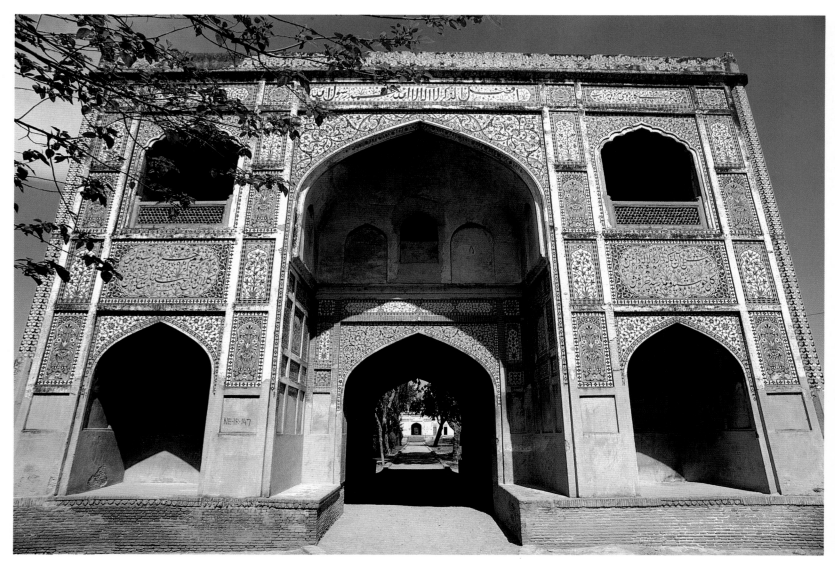

Punjab and ransack Lahore; and, if the Fates smiled, win themselves possession of that Pearl. Strategically the place was vital to the city's defence: and so Sher Shah Suri — the usurper who died regretting he had not annihilated Lahore and with it the worry of it — ordered Rohtas Fort to be built there. He did not fear — but he wanted to be ready for — the return of Humayun, Babur's son, whom he had deposed. And he wanted to protect his newly-built Great Trunk Road to the Indus — an earlier version of today's — from the Ghakkars who roamed the valley and, incidentally, favoured his enemies, the Mughals.

The excellence of the siting is self-evident: for the panoramic view of the hills to the north and the pass and the adjacent plain; for the river at the gate; and for the ravines behind. Even today there's no easy approach, unless by helicopter; and indeed within the fort there's little enough when you arrive. Even the later Mughals tented there. But more than four kilometres of such fortifications scrambling over the difficult hills, contoured by them, make an unforgettable sight.

Suri had ordered that the fort should be invincible, and was so enraged with the architect's first design that he ordered him beheaded. He was persuaded to give the man a second chance, but was himself dead in battle before the work was finished — ten years after it began. Nonetheless the final massiveness and solidity must surely have satisfied the most outrageously demanding military mind.

Despite the sixty-eight tower bastions and twelve huge gates it is the sandstone walls they fortify which dominate. Their height varies from thirty-three to sixty feet, according to the lie of the land, and their thickness — depending on the number of defensive terraces — can exceed twelve metres. Most of the circumference is double-, or triple-terraced, with staircases linking the different levels. Galleries within the walls provide for storage and accommodation.

Above: Remarkable for its faience mosaic and fine calligraphy, the seventeenth-century entrance is all that remains of Lahore's Gulabi Bagh pleasure garden. It was founded by an admiral of the Mughal fleet who blew himself to death when firing an English-made gun presented by Emperor Shah Jahan.

Opposite: Typical of Lahore's notable Victorian-Mughal architecture, Aitcheson (Chief's) College is today the most expensive educational institution in Pakistan.

Inside, a cross wall, 533 metres long, separates a citadel area from the rest, and within this a further enclave secures the highest point of the fort for the commander.

Maybe simply because it was there Rohtas Fort never had to withstand a siege; but anyway events diverted military action elsewhere. In Jahangir's reign the only interesting reference to the mighty fortress noted that while passing through it the emperor enjoyed some particularly good partridge.

The Salt Range, at whose feet Rohtas sits, lays bare 600 million years of earth's history. It is named for enormous deposits of rock salt left behind by seas that receded or evaporated that long ago. At Khewra these deposits have been mined for longer than man can remember, and a visit to its huge caves of what looks like chiselled marble — with their underground lakes and wells of saline water — is an enduring tourist attraction. At Kalabagh too there are large deposits of pure salt. The area also possesses large quantities of coal (worked at Dandot and Makerwal) gypsum and other minerals.

The landscape of this range is varied and fascinating — a barrier terrain that contrasts strongly with both the plain southward and the mountains to the north. Barren, exposed, red rock alternates with terraces fertile with seasonal crops and fruit orchards in the folds of hills that average about 2,300 feet in height — although in Sarghoda district the range reaches twice that elevation, making summers there very pleasant.

Alexander the Great came this way *en route* to his showdown battle with the defiant King Porus. The Macedonian had to outwit his enemy to get across the Jhelum unopposed, and so defeated him in battle — despite Porus's 200 battle elephants, which terrified Alexander's horses. But the Asian king's defiance and courage won Alexander's esteem.

'How would you be treated?' he asked his vanquished foe through an interpreter.

'Like a king,' was the level reply.

'That I would do for my own sake,' Alexander told him, 'what for yours?'

'It is enough,' said Porus.

His kingdom was restored as soon as he swore allegiance, and Porus remained loyal to Alexander until his death.

Crossing the Jhelum on the road from Lahore today lacks the romance of Alexander's crossing, but it has its own drama. Traffic can be dense on this section of highway, and the enormous transporters, trucks, buses and other vehicles all seem to be vying for first-past-the-post points. The earlier British road-and-rail bridge, nearly two kilometres long, crosses the river nearby. Alexander is said to have crossed the river with all his army not far to the south of it, at a time when the waters were rising.

Jhelum town, across the bridge, is of ancient foundation but acquired real status only after 1849 when the British took the area out of Sikh control and built one of their military cantonments there. Today Jhelum is an important Pakistan Army base. It is also an excellent place to stretch one's legs on a *charpoy* and take stock of the journey — and a tea and a *roti* or two — before going on to Rawalpindi and Islamabad 120 kilometres up the road.

Previous page top: Customers examine fine silks and brocades from China and the Far East in the comfort of a Lahore drapery. Bottom: Finely-worked filigree gold jewellery in Lahore goldsmith's shop is sold by weight, no matter how intricate the craftsman's work.

Opposite left: Ironing a finished handwoven masterpiece of carpet making for the export market.

Opposite: Lahore craftsman begins to weave a carpet from a coded numbered design handed down from the time that Emperor Shah Jahan developed the city as a carpet-making centre of renown. The code is called out by the master weaver.

Opposite: Dancing dervishes at an evening celebration in the streets of Lahore.

Here, on the north side of the Salt Range, is that confusion of rocky ridges, basin plains and 'badland' troughs and gullies dramatically eroded and dissected by streams, which is known as the Potwar Plateau. Another spread of intriguing country, this holds what is both oldest and newest in all Pakistan.

Here, white built amid the luxurious green, the strikingly modern capital city, Islamabad, stands where, millions of years past, mankind's ancestors left their bones to fossilize. In the same place only a few score thousand years ago Stone Age man flourished. Today the tools he used are not uncommon finds in the region, and British archaeologists are said to have identified the site of a 30,000-year-old house. Over the last 2,000 years, by contrast, man has found it hard to tame this environment, and the plateau has served mainly as a highway for invaders bound for the Punjab and the rich cities to the east. Only the Ghakkars — believed by some scholars to be a pre-Aryan people — really made it their own.

Islamabad and Rawalpindi are often talked of as twin cities. True, they're adjacent and they work together: their interdependence nowhere clearer than in the twice-daily races between the mini-buses carrying workers from the relative cheapness of the older city's residential areas to work in the giant government and business complexes of the new, and back again. But these twins actually resemble each other about as much as the proverbial chalk and cheese. Foster parent and child describes their relationship better.

Rawalpindi — 'Pindi for short — is certainly of ancient foundation; but nothing remains to show it. Mongols destroyed the older city and today's important regional centre dates from a Ghakkar chief's rebuilding in the fourteenth century. Even of this nothing has been left for the twentieth century to see — outside the rambling, unplanned bazaars of the old quarter. These though, for their traders and the buyers of their varied wares, the range of goods they display, and some evocative old buildings, richly reward a visit.

From the middle of the nineteenth century, after a period of Sikh control, Rawalpindi was developed by the British. They built an unusually large cantonment with typically tidily regimented, rectilinear lines of dwellings and offices that contrast vehemently with the random, lived-in sprawl of the older areas.

At Independence 'Pindi became headquarters of the Pakistan Army, with appropriate ordnance factories, training establishments and regimental depots. It quickly emerged as a centre of importance for the whole region; not just for the Potwar Plateau but for the valleys leading north into the hills past Taxila to Abbotabad and Manshera, for the oilfields of the plateau, and for Azad (Free) Kashmir.

In 1958, when it was decided to transfer the national capital from Karachi to somewhere more central with a better climate, the Islamabad site commended itself not least because Rawalpindi, with its large population, military installations and ready communications facilities, was there, ideally suited to act as foster parent. In fact, during the move — from 1961-3 — Rawalpindi served temporarily as capital of Pakistan.

Islamabad's master plan was drawn up by a Greek firm of architects, Doxiadis, as a triangle with its apex to the north-west, under the Margalla Hills, and its base to the south. The grid layout of the city

Opposite: Shrine to Sikhs throughout the subcontinent, the garlanded Lahore tomb, or Samadhi, of the greatest of the Sikh dynasty to rule Punjab, Ranjit Singh. His ashes are held in the largest of the lotus-shaped urns. The shrine draws a constant stream of pilgrims.

designates specific areas as government, diplomatic, and industrial sectors — each having its own shopping, recreation, and other amenities. The plan is that eventually Rawalpindi should be absorbed within the limits of the capital.

A first-time visitor will be struck by the tranquil beauty of Islamabad's setting in the lee of the steep, craggy Margalla hills; by the unexpected all-round verdure, and in it the glistening white blocks of modern buildings; and then quickly by the Shah Faisal mosque, with its four 300-foot rocket-like minarets at the corners, pointing the mind unmistakably to God.

The prayer hall, representing an eight-sided desert tent, is carried on four gigantic, concrete girders. Designed by the Turkish architect Vadat Dalokay the mosque was the US$50-million gift of Saudi Arabia. With a design capacity of 100,000 worshippers the builders of this superb structure must be justified in claiming it's the world's largest mosque.

Beneath it a two-storey building houses the Islamic Research Centre, a library, museum, Press Centre, lecture hall, and other components of the Islamic University.

The situation of Islamabad and Rawalpindi — in Punjab, but close to Baluchistan and the Northern Territories — makes them incomparable bases for touring. In their immediate vicinity is an endless variety of memorable walks and drives, and very little further out, higher, are more of nature's wonderlands: the Murree hills and the Galis.

It was the pines and deodars on their steep flanks that endowed the Murree Hills with that marvellously cool, refreshingly green and fragrant ambience that barracks-stale British officers and their wives from Rawalpindi so craved when they first developed this region with weekend-leave stations. The charm is undiminished still.

It isn't just the breath-of-paradise cool after the stifling heat of the towns. The views are stupendous. Probing ever steeply upwards like endlessly curious, prying snakes, the roads twist round one bend after another discovering more and more ranged hills. Most of their flanks are forested, but not uniformly. Some are bald in places, craggy, or green-stubbled as if needing a shave. The result is that exciting feeling everywhere that the hills live — are really a gigantic, muscular animal, sprawled sleeping under the cover of the trees. Villages perch in the sun on spurs hard by patches of more vivid, cultivated green.

Murree itself — 7,350 feet above sea level — is roughly two hours drive out of Islamabad and the most developed of the stations: largely because until 1876 it was used as the Punjab government's summer headquarters, with roads, hotels, and shopping facilities to match its status.

After 1876 Murree continued to grow, with the building of the road to Muzaffarabad and beyond to Kashmir, and the increased traffic this brought in its train. Nowadays government lodges and private houses exploit all conceivable building sites on the slopes. Murree's popularity shows no sign of decline.

Beyond Murree are the Galis — hill-stations so named from a dialect word meaning 'lane' — strung like a chain across the hills to Abbottabad. Most popular is Nathiagali, 8,200 feet above sea level, thirty-two kilometres north of Murree. Immediately north-east of this idyllic situation are the green slopes of Miran Jani, 9,000 feet high. Far beyond, but visible on a clear day, is the snow-bound majesty of Nanga Parbat — so lovely it seems to float above the pine-, chestnut-, oak- and maple-covered ridges that fold around Nathiagali. With such views it's easy to see why this is famous trekking and riding country.

Murree and the Galis are easily accessible from Islamabad and are the best known reach of the great Hazara Valley they adorn. But they by no means exhaust its interest. Hazara isn't all low hills clothed with pines, firs, deodars, rich grass, fat crops, colourful wild flowers, villages by sparkling streams under cloudless skies and views down valleys of high, distant, snow-capped mountains. Desolate, bleak, dry, barren stony creeks and sheer crags are found there. But they're not unwelcome. They underscore the perfection of the rest.

Eastwards is Jammu-Kashmir. For reasons entirely to do with their own interest the British, after the first Sikh war (1845-6), sold the immense, idyllic kingdom of Kashmir to a Hindu Raja. The quite unforeseen but, for Pakistan, traumatic consequence was that a century later, as the subcontinent braced itself for the sometimes agonising implications of partition the seventy-seven per cent Muslim population of the princely state of Jammu and Kashmir found themselves under a non-Muslim ruler, by whose sole fiat they were declared part of India.

For the founders of Pakistan it was an appalling betrayal of the principle on which Independence and Partition were based: that the majority will should be respected. Pakistani tribesmen tried to force the issue but were inevitably expelled by the Indian military. In time a cease-fire line, now referred to as the 'line of control', was established under United Nations auspices. It left the bulk of Kashmir in Indian hands.

'Azad' (Free) — north-western — Kashmir is controlled by Pakistan. It is the least known part of Pakistan's north, but one of the most strikingly and dramatically lovely. Easily reached too; although sadly it has the drawback of the 'line of control'. Tourists are allowed no nearer to it than sixteen kilometres.

Above Muzzafarabad, the administrative capital — close to the border with Hazara — are marvellous mountain views: ranks of ridges, rough and sharp, like Stone Age spearheads, neatly arranged, edges up for inspection, under the sky; streams like hairline fractures quicksilvering the relief of valleys; cataracts down a 3,000-foot gorge to the Jhelum catching and flashing back blindingly the sun. In the upper valley, too, there are lovely walks in thick pine forests, across wooden suspension bridges, above chalets like air vents snug on the slopes.

There are other rivers — the Neelum and the Punch the main ones. Their valleys too are beautiful — and in winter their weather dramatically changeable. From the end of November until March the region is held in a vice-like grip of ice. At this time, out of a sky of such immaculate blue that despite the keen edge of air off the enveloping, ice-harshened ridges you exult just to be alive, a cloud can form that within minutes fills a whole valley, turning it and the day suddenly grey.

Then, quickly as it came, the fog is gone — only for heavy and sullen, darker clouds to bear down. In no time your chalet refuge may be the plaything of a demented hailstorm. Shafts of lightning cleaving the darkness reveal the depths of the rock-strewn valley, followed almost

Above: Colourful garlands are popular for weddings and other celebrations.

instantly by explosions of thunder that reverberate endlessly round the walls of the mountain arena, unwilling to be quiet until they're overwhelmed by a more shattering detonation, as a fork of silver fire is plunged into the valley floor and a thunderbolt strikes an outstanding tree. Then the snow whirls white in the darkness and the whole world seems to creak and groan for the lost sun.

Carcasses of stricken pines can be seen on walks. Excursions on foot here are marvellous after March and before November, but they're not recommended during the high heat of June to August.

Westwards from Islamabad the Great Trunk Road quickly leads into a range of history remarkable even in Pakistan. Less than thirty-two kilometres from the capital the Margalla Pass is gateway to a 5,000-year spread of history unmatched even in this richly historic land.

It begins, briefly but emphatically, four kilometres beyond the Pass at the new Stone Age site of Sarai Khola. Precious little — it must be said — remains for the lay person to see. But 'digs' here — one kilometre from the road where today's men hurtle heedlessly by in their twentieth-century chariots — have proved that this valley supported man for more than a thousand years almost 2,000 years before, a few kilometres away on the other side of the road, Taxila and the famous Gandhara civilization it represents were even begun.

At Sarai Khola three levels of occupation were found. They covered roughly the period 3500 — 2200 BC. The lowest, oldest level revealed red burnished handmade pottery, stone axes and smaller stone and bone tools. The next occupants shared the life-style of the pre-Indus Valley civilization inhabitants of Amri and Kot Diji in Sind. In the more recent levels *terra cotta* bangles and female figurines, chert implements and wheel-made pottery, paste beads and copper pins were uncovered. And many intact graves.

And then, across the road: Taxila.

Three ancient trade routes, carrying the bulk of the traffic that passed overland between Hindustan, western and central Asia met in this exceptionally fertile and — for the period — densely populated valley of Takshasila: better known ever since Alexander the Great invaded it as Taxila.

The valley is eighteen kilometres long and eight wide and runs between two spurs of the Murree hills, shut off to the east by the Murree Hills themselves but wide open to the west. The convergence of major trade routes in such a place led naturally to the founding, by successive rulers, of cities to guard the western approach. These flourished: so well that more traffic was attracted, from all quarters. Taxila became, like another Rome, a place to which all roads led. The crucial importance of the trade routes was underlined later: for when the traffic along them declined, so did Taxila.

In the sixth century BC when the first Taxila (now called Bhir Mound) was built, the valley fell within the vast Persian empire of Cyrus the Great, near its northeastern limits: in a favoured part of the *satrapy* (province) called Gandhara. That first Taxila city was prosperous. It lasted more than 300 years, and during that time became, like Pushkalavati (modern Charsadda) to the west, an important centre of provincial administration.

In layout it was random — like a modern Pakistan town's old quarter, with rambling streets of low, flat-roofed houses built of mud-covered stone looking inward to courtyards with soakpits for refuse. There were no wells, because the water table was too low to reach; but the river was nearby.

On the credit side it boasted the most famous University of south Asia, which attracted students from all India to its courses in law, history, philosophy and theology, social, political and military science, medicine, the arts — and elephant husbandry. An important Grammar of Sanskrit was composed here; and here developed the alphabet of what was to become the script of Gandhara.

In 326 BC Alexander the Great was right royally entertained in this first city. He had studied under Aristotle, and he spent many weeks at Taxila University discussing philosophy with the naked ascetics of the place. It is thought that he may even have met there the future emperor of India, Chandragupta Maurya, who ascended the throne at Taxila soon after Alexander's visit.

Chandragupta's grandson — the famous Ashoka — was Viceroy in

Below: Pakistan's Gandhara culture, where Buddhist and Greek traditions intermingled, created its own art form with many different representations of Buddha, such as this one from Lahore Museum's Gandharan collection.

Right: Stone carving of Buddha from Gandhara, with followers in votive supplication.

Above: Considered one of the world's greatest works of art, Lahore Museum's 'Fasting Buddha' holds pride of place in its Gandharan collection.

Taxila before himself becoming emperor in 273 BC. Soon thereafter, he sponsored the spread of Buddhism to such effect that Gandhara became a Buddhist Holy Land, attracting large numbers of pilgrims to its numerous monasteries, shrines and *stupas*. The great *stupa* (burial mound) of Dharmarajika — the oldest uncovered in Taxila valley — was probably the work of Ashoka, built to hold genuine relics of Buddha.

Fifty years after Ashoka died the north of modern Pakistan was invaded by Bactrian Greeks — descendants of the troops Alexander the Great appointed to colonise northern Afghanistan (Bactria) in his name. In 180 BC they built their own Taxila city (called today Sirkap) only a kilometre from the original — in which a century and a half earlier Alexander himself had relaxed and talked philosophy. But only a century after that second city of Taxila was built first Scythians from Afghanistan and then, in AD 20, Parthians from Persia took control of the area: each in turn occupying the Bactrian Taxila (Sirkap).

What remains of its five-kilometre city wall — six-metres thick and up to thirty feet high — tells the story: Bactrian Greek — beautifully tidy building — at the bottom, then Scythian, then Parthian on top. The differences are instructive.

In AD 30 a powerful earthquake devastated the region and the Parthians had to rebuild much of the city. They followed the old city plan and built on its foundations: so that the layout the visitor sees today is what would have been seen by Christ's Apostle, Thomas the Doubter, who came here in AD 40 during the reign of the Parthian king Gondophares (who — tradition says — gave him an audience).

The wide main street, most of a kilometre in length, runs north-south and was lined with shops interspersed with Buddhist shrines — many of them with living accommodation. Two-storey private houses stood behind, with up to twenty rooms per storey, all built about the central courtyard. Nearly every block had its Buddhist or Jain *stupa*, with gilded dome and crowning umbrella. Exquisitely made gold and silver ornaments, copper vessels, farmer's tools, surgical instruments, cult objects (female fertility deities — Greek and Buddhist), bronze offering stands, censers, votive tanks, bronze mirrors, copper and bronze inkpots and other domestic articles unearthed at the site show the marvellous sophistication of this ancient city. A wide range of the finds is on display in Taxila's excellent museum.

High on the hillside opposite the south gate there's the tragic Kunala *stupa*. Ashoka had a son, Kunala, whose eyes were of such beauty that his stepmother wanted him. Angered because he refused her advances the woman sent an order, under Ashoka's seal, that the young man's eyes should be put out. Kunala's men were unwilling, but he insisted his father's command must be obeyed. Ashoka had the woman executed.

A third Taxila city — now called Sirsukh — was founded three kilometres north-east of Sirkap, about AD 80. This was the regional capital of the Kushan king Kanishka, whose forces — originally from north-west China — had invaded and overthrown the Parthians some twenty years before. With Kanishka they became ardent Buddhists and founded new monasteries all over the ancient region of Gandhara: enlarging, redecorating, gilding, and painting those already there from the days of Ashoka. By the fifth century AD Gandhara counted literally thousands of Buddhist *stupas* and monasteries within its borders.

In Taxila Valley almost every hilltop was crowned with a Buddhist shrine. Within a radius of ten kilometres the remains of fifty have been identified. Best preserved are the *stupa* and monastery at Jaulian. Even though the finest statues have been moved to the safety of museums, many remain to impress the visitor.

In and around courts on two levels the richly ornamented votive *stupas* and delightfully varied Buddha and Bhodisattva images — with attendants, elephants and lions about them — surround the main *stupa* while naked Greek Atlantes strain to support the beams above. Adjacent is the monastery: strikingly simply but solidly built, with cells and community rooms ordered about a central courtyard. Nothing is more

Above: Student at Lahore art college paints Lahore Museum in distant background.

impressive than the walls. Fifteen hundred years old they stand perfectly straight, tall, strong, true. They project an ancient, an immortal, ideal of beauty. For the turbulence of so many and such diverse peoples and cultures — invading, intermingling, building, being brought down and replaced by yet others through all those centuries — was not without its unique recompense.

By a kind of osmosis, artists trained in quite different traditions and cultures affected each other's work: with totally unexpected outcome. Eastern and western art forms, subjects and techniques, cross-fertilising, created the wonder of a new, 'Gandhara art' so vigorous that it flourished for five centuries, and so dynamic that it influenced artistic expression in central and southern Asia and in China itself. Today great museums worldwide pride themselves on possession of Gandhara sculptures, in which Buddhist subjects and Asian ideals are expressed with Greek love of representation. Buddha himself is for the first time anywhere portrayed — not just symbolically represented — and in narrative sequences that tell stories of his life and of how he helped those in need. Taxila museum is of course one of the best places in the world to admire these master works, but Lahore, Karachi and Peshawar museums too have many that are outstanding.

Despite new invaders after the third century Chinese Buddhists continued to visit Gandhara for 500 more years — and Tibetans down to the sixteenth century AD. But political unrest, aggravated by periodic floods and earthquakes deterred trade. So, finally, ancient Taxila declined.

In the tenth century Hinduism had seen a revival under the Shahis, but it was short-lived. In 1001 Mahmud of Ghazni emerged from the Afghan Hills to defeat the Shahi king, Jayapal, near Peshawar. Mahmud brought Islam to the northern Punjab: followed this way 500 years later by Babur on his way to found the Mughal dynasty and empire. Babur's descendants too came and went through Gandhara, to and from their periods of rest and recreation in Kashmir. The eighteenth and nineteenth centuries saw Sikhs and British scurrying backwards and forwards all through this region, contending for control.

So much history in one place — and yet still incomplete. Thirty kilometres down this historic road is the turning to the Tarbela Dam, one of the most spectacular engineering projects of the twentieth century.

The Tarbela is the biggest earth-filled dam in the world — more than three times the size of the Aswan, on the Nile. With a design capacity of 3,500 megawatts it was built to generate more electricity than any other similar structure. The basin can store an amount of water equivalent to an entire winter season flow of the Indus.

The undertaking called for creation of a ninety-one-kilometre-long lake behind a barrier 2.7 kilometres wide. The views from the surrounding hills are exhilarating, especially of the overspill driving down the two 380-foot spillways and plunging thunderously over into the catchment pools below.

A masterwork of twentieth-century engineering the Tarbela Dam is thus at once a new and worthy landmark in the 5,000-year history of a remarkable region, and an emphatic symbol of the enduring economic importance of Pakistan's Five Rivers province.

6 The Vale and the Mountains

*'Who today is disgraced
Tomorrow will be lost.'*
— (Pashtu proverb)

The Indus at Attock marks off Punjab from Pakistan's most northerly and scenically dramatic province, named — simply, yet with accrued heavy overtones of high adventure, dashing gallantry and romance — North-West Frontier Province, NWFP.

Apart from the Vale of Peshawar which, with Taxila, was seen by invaders as the first place to plunder on their way into the subcontinent, it is a region of mountains, many formidably great and tolerating only rare, fabled passes, and of valleys, some bare, others outstandingly lovely, cut by sharp waters and frequented by ancient travellers' ways.

It is also the land of the Pathans.

Still strongly tribal, for centuries the Pathans have dominated the northwest of what is today Pakistan. More than anything else their fiercely independent spirit accounts for the region's endemically turbulent and — in the telling at least — romantic character. The Pathan tribesman stands formidable in the folklore of every race that has had to do with him.

His dominant loyalty is to his heritage. centering on his tribal lore — *Puktunwali* — a strict code of behaviour that operates side by side with the Qu'ran. Honour, hospitality, revenge are its watchwords, and the *Jirga* — the tribal assembly — the judge of main issues.

Nobody can say with certainty where the Pathan originally came from but their character — respected perforce by friend and foe — undoubtedly takes much of its huge pride and rugged, independent toughness from the mountains in which they live.

Winston Churchill, who served with the British Army in Pathan country, remarked that their qualities seemed to harmonise with their environment. Every male Pathan, he said, was a warrior, a politician, and a theologian — a life he considered 'full of interest'.

An age that sees women as people with rights equal to men's may wonder whether Pathan women would agree with Churchill. Pathan society is unashamedly a male dominion. The women seem born to bear children, do all the housework, till the field — and hand the men ammunition in battle.

Already at Attock, on the Punjab side of the Indus, the fortress built by Akbar shows how little that great Mughal trusted the tribesmen on the other, restless shore. In his case it was a matter of 'once bitten twice shy'. His half-brother Hakim Mirza, ruler of Kabul, had crossed the river in an attempt to possess Lahore and, having failed, beat a speedy retreat back home. Akbar led the punitive expedition himself, ferrying his army across the Indus in 1581 and ordering construction of the Attock fort. Eventually it was just one of several he built in the area, but even Akbar never really controlled the western shore.

Attock castle is still used by the Pakistan Army. It dominates the point where the southward-bound Indus begins its final confinement in a gorge at the western end of the Salt Range — sharp-ridged and startlingly vari-coloured with ochres, reds, greens and glistening-with-salt white.

The gorge ends 160 kilometres to the south at Kalabagh — a romantic place of cliffs and flamboyant colours and mud-brick houses on tiny terraces clinging to the walls of the gorge on top of one another. There the river again swings out wide and open across the Punjab plain,

Previous pages: Pathan warrior guards his tribal homelands in the Khyber Pass.

Above: Salt bricks used to build a mosque deep in the bowels of the Punjab's Salt Range glow luminously in the dark of a Khewra salt mine.

bringing it a fertility in green that contrasts vividly with the stark, surrounding desert.

Not far north of Kalabagh Genghis Khan was baulked by a defeated enemy, Jalalludin of Khwarizm, who spurred his horse to a spectacular jump off the cliff into the river. The Khan was impressed. But not enough to emulate the feat.

In this colourful, fabled setting a new dam is to be built — partly to replace the capacity that will be lost as, inevitably, the dams at Tarbela and Mangla on the Jhelum silt up.

Downstream from Kalabagh the Indus is already irrigating land in both the NWFP and Punjab via the Chasma barrage and the 270-kilometre-long Right Bank Canal project. This aims to make more than 2,000 square kilometres fertile: 1,400 of them in the Derajat — the area around Dera Ismail Khan (D. I. Khan).

Westward of D. I. Khan runs another of those ancient trade routes which linked the prehistoric and Indus Valley civilization peoples with their contemporaries on the Iranian plateau and beyond. Many archaeological sites mark the route. The nearest to D. I. Khan, twenty-

two kilometres to the north, is the pre-Indus Valley settlement at Rahman Deri. The typical grid layout and ancient brick walls date from 3,200 BC.

Those ancient trade routes entered Afghanistan via the Gomal Pass, in the extreme south of Waziristan — one of Pakistan's officially-designated 'Tribal Areas'.

Unlike Pakistan's three other provinces the NWFP has two administrations. One, identical with the system used throughout the rest of the country, is for what are referred to as the 'settled' areas. The other is for the eleven Federally Administered Tribal Areas (FATAS) that lie along the international border (Durand Line) with Afghanistan. These are a legacy of the buffer zone the British established to safeguard their precious Indian Empire. The special administrative status they enjoy today aims to protect their ancient and varied cultural identities, and tourism is discouraged.

Seen from a distance this western borderland, with its jagged mountain peaks and steep gorges, is spectacular — cruel and merciless, hard and bare. In fact Waziristan has been called the place where God

Above: Majestic ruins of the massive Rohtas Fort built to guard the northern approaches to Lahore on the orders of Sher Shah Suri who was killed in battle before its completion.

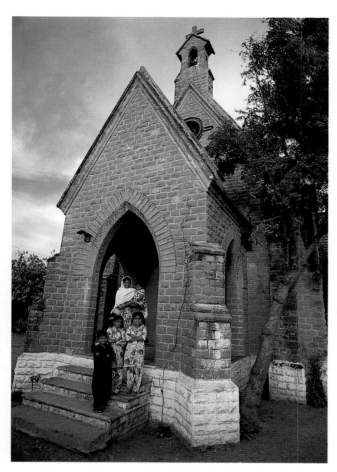

Above: One of Pakistan's minority Christian families at the parish church of St. John, Khewra.

dumped the lumber of creation — all the rock and stone he didn't want.

Yet those who know it love Waziristan. They say the sun fills the desolation with colour, and makes the rock plants wonderfully fragrant, aromatic. Wherever survival is possible surprisingly large communities of people live among these gaunt, rocky landscapes.

The river valleys are less bleak. The main ones are the Khurram and the Tochi furthest south — which deposit a rich silt that yields wheat, barley, maize, rice and sugarcane in the region about Bannu, west of Kalabagh — and the Kohat, which has the most fertile valley, and produces a similar range of crops, plus substantial quantities of melons.

Kohat town has long been important as a market and garrison centre. It was from the cantonment there that Pathan tribesmen kidnapped the young English girl, Molly Ellis, in 1923, releasing her later unharmed. A *cause celebre* at the time it did nothing to moderate the lively Victorian lore of danger and extravagant adventure that still attaches to the name of the North-West Frontier and the Pathan.

Two place names above all others are associated with them: their capital Peshawar, and the Khyber Pass.

The main approach to the provincial capital, Peshawar, is from the east, via the Vale named for it. Though surrounded by mountains it is culturally one with Taxila valley. They were twin hubs of ancient Gandhara.

Driving through the Vale today one is conscious only of its loveliness and of its modern wealth — farms and orchards and, closer to the city, factories. The region produces some of the world's finest plums, pears and peaches and abundant cash crops of tobacco, rice and sugarcane.

But the heartbeat of ancient Gandhara — commercial and cultural crossroads of east and west two centuries before Alexander the Great was born — is still felt here, as at Taxila.

At least 700 years before the Kushan king Kanishka made Peshawar capital of Gandhara in the second century AD that honour was held by the exotically named Pushkalavati — the Lotus City — nineteen kilometres north of Peshawar, outside modern Charsadda. This Lotus City was ruled by its own king before it ever came under the sway of the Persian overlord, Cyrus the Great. And even under the Persians Pushkalavati, like its sister city Taxila east of the Indus, kept a considerable measure of independence.

Like Taxila it was an important and prosperous administrative centre, spreading its jumble of narrow, winding streets and alleyways, bazaars, and public offices across an area of twenty-five hectares under the protection of its citadel.

When, two centuries after Cyrus carved it out, Alexander the Great conquered the mighty Persian empire and set about extending his own, Pushkalavati showed its strength and character. The Gandharan capital held out against Alexander's second-in-command, Hephaistion, for thirty days before it capitulated.

There were still two centuries of life left in the city after Alexander the Great's passage. But then it suffered the same fate as the first Taxila. The Bactrian Greeks came, built 'their' Pushkalavati — at the same time as they built 'their' Taxila, and with a strikingly similar groundplan — and left the older foundation to die.

Opposite: Twisting series of hairpins forms the switchback road through the Salt Range to Khewra salt mines.

Above: Smiling Pathan youngster of the NWFP.

In Pushkalavati's case that didn't happen. Although only a seventy-foot mound called Bala Hisar (High Fort) remains, excavators have shown it was occupied for more than twenty centuries — from the sixth century BC to the eighteenth AD. No fewer than fifty-two different levels of occupation have been found. Quite probably the mound seen today is what's left of the citadel that was the keystone of the resistance Alexander's army encountered twenty-three centuries ago.

Like Taxila valley the Vale of Peshawar is packed with places of historic and religious importance. Three of them are 'musts' for anyone seriously interested in knowing what has gone into the making of today's Pakistan, and what its past has already given to the world.

First is the monastery of Takht-i-Bahi.

Enormous quantities of superb sculpture have come from mounds thickly scattered over wide areas of the Vale of Peshawar, north of Pushkalavati (Charsadda), but easily the most impressive complex commands a spur 600 feet above the plain in a tortured *cul-de-sac* called Takht-i-Bahi — 'Enthroned Spring'. It is the nearest-to-complete Buddhist monastery in Pakistan. Monks lived, worked and prayed in it from the first to the seventh century AD.

Massive walls surround the sanctuary. Inside, against the hill, the principal *stupa* stands in a courtyard lined on three sides with chapels — each of which once contained statues of the Buddha, some more than thirty feet high. Steps lead down to another courtyard full of the remains of votive *stupas* and more chapels.

To the north is the two-storey monastery, with monks' cells ranged round three sides. Originally these were plastered and painted different colours and had wooden doorposts and lintels, decorated with carvings. Each also had its own window and niches for the monk's lamp and personal belongings.

The setting is superb. The wide views of the plain incline the mind to meditation. Enjoyed for years they must have bred profound peace of mind.

Next, thirty-two kilometres to the east, is Shahbaz Garhi. One of the greatest kings of all time still speaks to humankind here — more than 2,000 years after his death. You may well leave this place conscious of being privileged to visit it — and perhaps praying not to forget.

Three centuries before Christ the main Afghanistan-India highway through Pushkalavati (Gandhara's capital at the time) went via Shahbaz Garhi where it met the incoming trade route from China and another Afghan highway that came in from the north. Shahbaz was thus an important rendezvous for travellers — and the perfect place, therefore, to broadcast royal proclamations. King Ashoka ordered that fourteen edicts should be carved into the smoothed surface of two rocks there in the local Gandhara script, Kharoshthi.

Ashoka prefaced these edicts by telling of his remorse for all the destruction and slaughter he had caused in war. Next he promised he would always be available to his subjects to hear their pleas — no matter how busy he might be when they called on him. Then he ordered honour to be shown to parents and family, forbade the slaughter of animals, noted the futility of many religious rites and urged self-control, respect and generosity as the best ways to gain merit. He commanded everyone

to show religious tolerance to those of other beliefs. He ordered hospitals to be founded to treat people and dumb animals, and medicinal herbs to be planted; fruit trees too along the roadside, and wells dug for travellers.

The ancient town of Shahbaz Garhi is gone. Ashoka's great stones stand, simply but well cared for on a mound a few hundred metres from the main road — monuments to a real king among men.

And then Hund on the west bank of the Indus — where the ancient Afghanistan-India highway through Pushkalavati and Shahbaz Garhi crossed over to Hazro and then Taxila on the eastern side. Until Akbar built the Grand Trunk Road Hund was the immemorial western gateway into India. The Indus here flows wide and shallow in summer and so is fordable. Alexander the Great's commander Hephaistion chose it as the place to build the bridge of boats by which his 50,000 men plus animals should march into the subcontinent in 326 BC. He was met the other side by the king of Taxila, come to surrender his arms, but with such pomp and circumstance there was nearly a bloody misunderstanding.

Hund was an important Buddhist shrine for centuries, and is among

Above: Ruins of a second-century sundial among the remains of the predominantly Buddhist city of Sirkap, at Taxila. Of Greek foundation, the city was visited by the Christian apostle, Thomas the Doubter, in AD 40.

Opposite: The Buddhist monastery of Jaulian at Taxila.

Above: Pottery on sale in Taxila town.

the many places in Gandhara where the Buddha was said to have lived in earlier incarnations. Then in AD 870 it became the Hindu Shahi capital until 1001, when Mahmud of Ghazni vowed he would drive the Hindus out of Gandhara. Here in Hund the Shahi king, knowing himself beaten, climbed on to his own pyre and immolated himself.

These Shahis were Turkish — former rulers of Kabul who came east to rule Gandhara when they were driven from Afghanistan. Their kingdom was wide: stretching from Gandhara to Multan in Punjab, up to Kashmir and across the Swat valley. And they were given a remarkably good press by the Arab Muslim scholar and historian Al-Biruni. 'In all their grandeur,' he says, 'they never slackened in the ardent desire of doing that which is good and right'. He called them men of sentiment and noble bearing.

Akbar built one of his Indus forts at Hund — intended to 'pacify' the Pathan. It hardly succeeded, but the walls are not wasted. Today they shelter a riverside village.

And so at last — via the Vale, following the traders, students, and pilgrims of nearly twenty centuries — into Peshawar.

Above: Taxila potter working on the delicate decoration of a finished pot.

Those traders brought luxury goods from China in the north east, from the Mediterranean in the distant west, from Central Asia and Persia, and from the south and far side of the Indian subcontinent. Following them came the scholars and the devout. Kanishka's espousal of Buddhism led to an immense Buddhist revival throughout Gandhara. The most splendid *stupa* in the empire stood in this city, built by Kanishka himself. Pilgrims from many places left accounts of it: 620 feet high, with thirteen carved wooden terraces and crowned by a mast bearing twenty-five gilded discs. Lightning struck several times and by the seventh century it was a ruin. The site is pointed out today in the middle of the enormous King's Mound (Shah-ji-ki-Dheri) cemetery. People, it seems, wanted to be buried in its shade.

Peshawar has seen more than its share of less peaceful visitors too: conquering Greeks, devastating Huns, the Ghaznavids overturning the Rajput rebuilding, followed later by the Mughals, Persians, Afghans, Sikhs, and finally the British. It was always strongly defended.

Until the middle of this century, old Peshawar was enclosed by a city wall entered by one of its sixteen gates. Now the massive Sikh-built

Above: Muslims of Pakistan's Shi'ite sect mark Ashura-i-Muharram.

Balahisar Fort (which must be one of the most 'unmissable' structures in any city in the country) dominates the area, unchallenged. Balahisar stands on the site of several ancient fortresses — notably Babur's built in 1530 — frowning down on the maze of old streets and alleys and bazaars which today are hearth and home to the spirit of Peshawar.

No need to say the old city's different quarters hammer out and cut and saw and mould and bake and clean and string and carve and offer for sale everthing from pottery and metalwork to basketry and blankets, jewellery (yes, gold and antique silver and fine stone) leathers, skins, birds and beads; fruit and shawls, hats and knives, electrical goods, grains, the Peshawar 'chappals' or sandals, belts, holsters, and — if you must — bandoliers.

And of course refreshments: fresh fruit and fresh fruit juices, crushed sugarcane and sweetmeats, tikkas, kebabs, and breads — and always tea.

But to list these is to describe practically every self-respecting bazaar in Pakistan. Only here in Peshawar, though, is the famed Qisa Khawani Bazaar (the 'Street of Story Tellers') — called by Sir Herbert Edwardes 'the Piccadilly of central Asia' — where travellers of yore regaled each other with tales of incredible journeys and the wonders they'd witnessed on the way, of foul deeds done and just recompense, of wisdom and (best-loved) of courage; or rested, listening to the professionals telling stories as they shared a bubbling hookah or sipped tea in the shade of a bazaar shopfront.

Peshawar has an important Mughal mosque, the Mahabat Khan. It's entered from the Andarshahr bazaar where, in medieval proximity, the long lines of jewellers shops display their rich wares. How, with such concentrated abundance, can there possibly be a living for them all, one wonders yet again? Obviously there is; and evidently a good one. Has the mosque to do with it? It's in their midst; the warp and weft of life. . . .

Above: Colourful banners during the annual Ashura-i-Muharram that marks the death of Hazrat Imam Hussain.

Mahabat Khan was twice governor of Peshawar region, under both Shah Jahan and his son Aurangzeb. The governor's mosque is worthy of that supreme period of Mughal building: not very large and now, perhaps, somewhat hemmed in by its surroundings; but with beautiful interior decoration of the main prayer hall and outside, above, three lovely fluted domes. The Italian soldier of fortune known as General Avitabile, who served the Sikhs during their period of control, used the minarets as gallows.

The Andarshahr bazaar leads into the main rallying point of the old city, the Chowk Yaadgar, with its monument to the heroes of the 1965 war with India. Most of the men gathered on one side of the square, where tourists park their cars, are Afghans. Traders move among them offering their wares — knives are prominent — but the main business is money-changing. The dealers are ready for big business. They have their safes with them by the kerb.

The houses here are of two or three storeys but they look tall — partly the effect of their narrow building, partly of the many finely carved wooden balconies adorning the upper floors and overhanging the crowded streets. Most are of unbaked brick set in wooden frames as a precaution against earthquake.

Something in the atmosphere of Peshawar is distinctive. Everywhere's convivial and intimate, relaxed, warm, and human. It gives Peshawar a different 'feel' from Lahore and Karachi. The breath of the Pass blows through it and with it the tough, fresh-air cameraderie of long-distance travellers. With little imagination you sense the 2,000-year-old tradition. It's in the stones.

The British Saddar (cantonment) on the other side of the railway lines is typical of its kind: with pleasantly wide streets, good buildings, gardens, parks and many trees. Best of the buildings is the old Victoria

Left: Interior of the seventeenth-century Mahabat Khan Mosque, last of Peshawar's Mughal mosques, named after a city Governor who served both Shah Jahan and Aurangzeb.

Memorial Hall — now an excellent museum, with one of the country's best collections of Gandhara art. Modern hotels are in this district: among them the famous Dean's — in the Colonial bungalow style of its sister hotels in Lahore (Faletti's) and Rawalpindi (Flashman's): popular with many tourists for their old-world atmosphere of sunny verandahs and attentive, uniformed staff.

To the west is modern Peshawar's pride: the University. Flanked by a bevy of other academic institutions — among them the now venerable Islamia college, the Academy of Rural Development, and the laboratories of the Council of Scientific and Industrial Research — it stands on a road once feared for its vulnerability to tribal raiding parties: the route to the Khyber.

West of the city it lies, this tormented meander of a way through the Sulaiman Hills that separate Pakistan from Afghanistan. It's by no means the easiest place to get through. The many waves of prehistoric immigrants and traders from the west never used it. They preferred the Gomal and the Bolan passes further south. Alexander the Great's general Hephaestion didn't use it. With at least half the Macedonian army in his charge — while Alexander led the rest in a dangerous flanking excursion through Swat — he followed the river Kabul, north of the Khyber.

Not until Peshawar became winter capital of the Kushan Empire in the second century AD did the Khyber, which gave direct access to the Kushan city, acquire favour. Peshawar made the Khyber important — not vice-versa.

Even then the Khyber, where the jinking hills dip to allow a way through that's a kilometre and a half wide in some places, and barely fifteen metres across in others, remained the hard way — fifty-six kilometres of toiling round and up and down and up the seemingly endless loops of physically hostile terrain. And always under the sharp watchful eyes — and so ever at the mercy — of the proud, marauding Pathan whose home it was. As it still is.

Fourteen centuries after Kanishka — about the time Elizabeth the First of England was starting to worry about the enormous armada of battleships the king of Spain was assembling against her — Akbar, the English queen's almost exact contemporary, made the Khyber more important by driving his Grand Trunk Road through it; so linking the new and old Mughal capitals, Delhi and Kabul.

But as at Attock, so here in the Khyber: the great Akbar failed to assert real control over the Pathans. He never managed to make the Pass really secure.

When the British came they paved their way through it and added forts and pickets to guard its whole length in the name of protecting the Empire from the Russians.

But on the ground the British could never relax their guard. They had to strike, and constantly renew, fresh deals with the Pathan, playing — and paying — one tribe off against another to maintain an always uneasy measure of control.

There were many fights between the British and the Pathans up and down the Pass even so; and many battles with Afghans in the various wars. It was a point of honour never to leave wounded men behind. Death by inches and hideous mutilation were the normal measure meted out — especially by the Pathan.

Above: Punjab worker enjoys a moment's relaxation with his hookah pipe.

'When you're wounded an' left on Afghanistan's plains,
An' the women come out to cut up what remains,
Jest roll to your rifle an' blow out your brains. . . .'

This was the urging of Kipling's soldier. Of course the British had their own punitive campaigns, and razed many a village to the ground. The Khyber was ever a bloody place: no one had illusions about that. That's why the very name cut like a knife to the romantic core of generations that knew almost nothing else about the country or its people.

Today's more cynical age is less ready to be stirred at the thought of men asking and giving no quarter in such a place; but that can take nothing away from the courage and character of the many men who were tested and proved in this vast, rock-bound arena.

There are marvellous views and much to see: from the forts — the Sikh Jamrud which marks its start, the Shagai, built by the British, and the Ali Masjid that guards the narrowest part of the gorge — past the mosque and the Sphola *stupa* (from which many fine Gandharan sculptures were recovered for display in Peshawar museum) to Landi Kotal, the 'smugglers' town' — where, having done enough, the stubbornly enchanting, twin-steam-engined railway ends, eight kilometres short of the border post at Torkham.

The real magic is worked by the mind's own caravan. There, stout merchants and lean pilgrims, urgent messengers and couldn't-give-a-

Above: Brass and copper bazaar in Peshawar.

damn adventurers, despairing refugees and footloose wanderers, professional travellers and contraband-bearing-brigands trudge, struggle, hurry or plod along the rock-edged trail — their wares, provisions, money, and all their hopes, carried on the backs of asses and camels, mules and horses, or piled on creaking carts. There too are the fresh young troopers out on a first (maybe last) picket duty, half the world from home; and above them, through the centuries, always — the armed, squatting, watching tribesmen breathing easily the dangerous air they alone were born to. And there always the sharp attacks and sharper reprisals.

The Khyber is by no means the only attraction of the area about Peshawar. Just as Islamabad provides access to the idyllic hill station resorts of Murree and the Ghalis, and further north and east to the Hazara Valley and Azad Kashmir, so Peshawar invites the traveller to explore northern valleys. The most accessible, and by far the richest in recorded history, is the prosperous valley of the river Swat. For many it is the most beautiful of Pakistan's numerous enchanting valleys.

It has its seasons, of course. But even when the source of its life, the

Above: Smiling shoeshine boys in the heart of Peshawar's old walled city.

river, is at its lowest before the spring thaw, when the blossom's no more than a hint of a flush about the leaf-bare trees in the cherry orchards along the way, when even the hardy go out into the sun blanket-wrapped and their shouts cut sharp on the air, and when only a blazing fire kept in all night emboldens you to bed — even at its chillest and least dressed the sun-loving Swat valley will soothe the most troubled spirit.

A Pathan poet said Swat was meant 'to give pleasure to kings' — though the record shows he did not mean just 'any old king'.

Alexander the Great for one had fierce fights at practically all the hill forts. The tribesmen learned to shut themselves up securely at his approach and then harry his rear. He personally collected a couple of arrows — one in the shoulder and one in the ankle — and had other adventures which included at least one narrow escape, in the assault on Massaga.

The great Mughals Babur and Akbar both suffered serious reverses trying to subdue Swat. And most recently the British — vividly reported by the young Winston Churchill — discovered that the Pathan didn't count them kings; or not king enough.

Above: Regimental crests set into the Khyber Pass mountainside are witness to its long history of turmoil.

Originally called Udyan (Garden) Swat justified the name, and still does. The lower valley in particular — as far as the capital Saidu Sharif — with its terraced fields, abundant fruit orchards and superb views of snow-capped mountains, seems enchanted. Beyond the capital the river is more constrained, more aggressive in narrow gorges, and the steep slopes of the valley walls bristle with pines. All of it is excellent climbing and walking country — for many the best in the world — and the fishing is highly praised. And what the thronging mountains further north are to mountaineers, Swat is to the devotees of history and archaeology: an endless store of challenge and reward.

The valley was inhabited by Stone Age communities 5,000 years ago. In 1700 BC invading Aryans fought a battle on the river banks and told the story of it in the *Rigveda* — the oldest existing Hindu scriptures (certainly dating from 1000 BC but probably older).

After Alexander fought his way through in 326 BC Ashoka the Mauryan came and made the whole valley Buddhist. And so it stayed for nearly 1,000 years — the evidence is in a thousand shrines liberally sprinkled everywhere as far along the upper valley as Bahrain, and happily collected in museums like those of Saidu Sharif and Chakdara.

During the next three centuries the Hindu Shahis dominated the region, perching their walled cities on hilltops all over the southern half of Swat. You see them from the road still. And then in 1001 Mahmud of Ghazni brought the message of Islam.

But there was no easy admission for anyone: Mahmud lost his greatly admired commander Kushal Khan in bitter fighting at Udegram, north of Saidu Sharif. And the Mughals came off worst in some bloody battles.

Then, apart from a brief period of unity under a charismatic nineteenth-century figure known as the Akund of Swat, the people of the valley generally went their own ways until, with British recognition of

Opposite: Bab-el-Kyber, gateway to the Khyber Pass in Pakistan's North-West Frontier Province, with Jamrud Fort in background.

the valley as a separate state in 1926, the Akund's grandson was recognised as ruler. Full integration into independent Pakistan came in 1969.

Swat is entered from the south at the Malakand Pass, described by Winston Churchill as 'a great cleft in the line of mountains'. On every side steep, precipitous hills are covered with boulders and stunted trees, confused, irregular. It's a busy and steep and winding way up: broad enough comfortably for one lane of traffic each way — uncomfortable indeed when the labouring truck or overcrowded mini-bus approaching you on the safe inside track is amazingly being overhauled on the bend by some young and determined descendant of Genghis Khan. The side where you fear to go over the edge is reassuringly fenced — till you realise why, every so often, there are gaps. . . .

There was fierce fighting at the fort on top of the hill in 1897. One thousand Sikh infantrymen under British officers held off ten times their number of tribesmen till reinforcements arrived. And there was more sharp action by the river the other side of the hill at Damkot — also now known as Churchill's Picket.

This is a steeply rising carbuncle of a hill on the north shore of the Swat with fabulous views from the top, up and down the valley and adjacent passes. And during the same Pathan uprising Winston Churchill, reporting for the London *Daily Telegraph* newspaper, squeezed every drop of *Boy's Own* excitement out of an action in which, as at Malakand Fort, the day was saved only by nick-of-time reinforcements.

That picket rock is awash with history. The Aryans who came in 1700 BC settled at its foot: and some of their graves have been uncovered and recovered.

For the first five centuries of the Christian era Buddhists lived there and in many other places in the neighbourhood, as the excavated *stupa* and monastery on the river side still show. In the eighth century the Turkish Hindus (Shahis) built one of their forts at the top and occupied it till the time of Mahmud of Ghazni's invasion in 1001 when it was burnt down — probably by Mahmud's men; but extensive remains of that Shahi building can be visited, from the top to the bottom of the hill. After that nobody else cared to use the place till the British came, late in the nineteenth century.

Across the road from the picket rock, occupied now by the Pakistan Army, is a fort the British built on foundations laid by Akbar in the sixteenth century. And as if that were not enough history on one small parcel of land there are Buddhist rock carvings too — 1,500 years old — down by the river. Just up the road Chakdara museum offers a small but most impressive display of Gandhara sculptures and other local artefacts.

Further upriver, on the southern shore, is Mount Ilam — a shrine sacred since prehistoric times to ethnic ancestors and local gods, and subsequently adopted as a holy place by Buddhists, Hindus and Muslims. It now seems most likely that this was that 'Mountain Without Birds' — Aornos — which was the scene of one of Alexander the Great's most admired victories.

Aornos was the supreme defensive citadel of the Swatis, who fled there from the Macedonian catapults and other war machines they'd

Opposite: The weekly Khyber Pass special steams into Peshawar station.

never seen before in the understandable confidence that Alexander could not reach them there. But the indefatigable Alexander spent three days felling nearby pinewoods and then erected a 500-metre-long ramp across the ravine that separated him from the Aornos citadel so that he could bring it within range of his catapults and arrows.

The subsequent bombardment terrified the defenders. They began to slip away under cover of dark as Alexander led his troops, with hoists and shoving, up the steep sides of the fortress rock until their numbers were enough to break the remaining defenders. It was counted a staggering feat of determination, enterprise, and generalship both among local rulers, who came spontaneously suing for peace, and even by the troops Alexander led — who were already convinced there was nothing their general could not do.

Beyond Saidu Sharif, the capital town, the going through Swat used to get quite a bit tougher than it is today. In fact, until the 1930s, when the administration of the Akund's grandson was developing the then separate state with roads and other public amenities, the traveller had to get either very wet or very weary to proceed beyond Mingora.

The walls of the valley there drive out sheer to the river and according to the season it was a climb up and over the rock or a wade through the water to go further. But the alternative — journey's end — would have been unthinkable for those who knew the little towns, tracks, and side valleys of Upper Swat.

Like Miandam — fifty-six kilometres beyond Saidu Sharif and 6,000 feet above the sea. Miandam basks in sun-filled mountain air awaiting the afternoon batches of visitors ecstatic under the so-close, so-distant, immovable peaks; or for sight of the day's first stirrers, out climbing up the way the streams come down from the snow-topped heights behind; or drawing in a day of still transparent views of steep-set, fairyland terraces and the deep valley beyond with a timely breath of summer night's cool across the verandahs and tea-table-laid lawns.

All around there are beautiful drives — crossing through the mountains to the Indus Gorge, or visiting Bahrain, Mingora or Kwazakhela for the bazaars and local colour. Many of the doors and beams and balconies of the houses are beautifully carved — an ancient tradition still alive.

The road to the head of the valley is normally closed outside the summer months. The gorge narrows and steepens considerably and the pine trees clothing its sides show unsuspected skills in their ability to find purchase for their roots. The road lacks a level. It rises and falls constantly — there right down by the churning water, here too many hundreds of feet above it, but always offering enticing views of the tall peaks to come.

Kalam, 6,800 feet above sea level, is where the Swat river is born, of the confluence of three rivers — the Ushu, Utrot and Gabral. Shingle roads follow their valleys to give trekkers long, breath-taking sight of 19,415-feet high Mount Falaksair ahead, and views of another peak that's 20,000 feet high — one of Pakistan's innumerable unnamed mountains.

To anyone who hasn't grasped the scale of Pakistan's north it's astonishing that a peak several thousand feet higher than Mont Blanc — at 15,772 feet the highest in the Alps — isn't even given a name. But it's

hardly surprising. Not easily reached from this point at the head of the Swat valley, but physically not far, is the galaxy of even greater mountains that is the crown of northern Pakistan.

In a narrow compass are five of earth's total of fourteen peaks above 26,250 feet; and more than sixty that exceed 23,000 feet. In such company it's no wonder that literally hundreds — many of them more than 19,500 feet high — go unnamed. They are marked, like Falaksair's mighty neighbour, by a dot on a map.

The Swat valley is prosperous largely because it sits plum in the middle of the best watered region of the country. To the west is Dir — its own west bounded by Afghanistan and the Hindu Kush. Eastwards, across the Indus, lies Hazara, the large territory best known for the hill stations of Murree and the Galis in the south.

This broad belt of country is deeply scored by the valleys of the Swat, Indus, and Jhelum rivers and their many tributaries. The valley sides vary greatly in height. None is less than 4,000 feet — the height of a mountain in Britain; others rise higher than the Alps, to 16,500 feet. Many of the valley people are pastoralists, the Gujars especially, and they exploit the varied grazing on the slopes by transhumant migration up and down the steep valley walls.

Whole villages move together: from their locked-up winter homes on the valley floors at around 2,000 feet above sea level to heights around 14,000 feet, completing the enormous climb by stages — through four or five 'temporary home' huts on the way to the top.

The valley sides are roughly terraced and cropped with maize, wheat and mustard according to season. But landslides are a constant threat — often destroying hard won homes and crops.

Kat Kala in Dir has been identified with Massaga, the most important town of the region when Alexander the Great captured it in 327 BC. Before

Top: Pathan warrior.

Above: Youngster making ammunition in the town of Darra Adamkhel.

Above: Gunsmith in Darra Adamkhel where firearms are made to order or sold straight over the counter.

the battle was won an assault bridge collapsed under the weight of men pressing to fight by Alexander's side. But they were lucky — the drop was not too great.

Curtius, the first-century AD biographer of Alexander, says that after envoys had returned to Massaga with the pardon they had been sent to obtain, the queen herself went down with a great train of noble ladies. They poured out libations of wine in golden bowls and the queen placed her child at Alexander's knees, obtaining not just pardon but the right to retain her royal title.

The historian says the clemency was attributed by some more to the charms of the queen's person than to pity for her misfortune, and notes, perhaps disingenuously, that her majesty later bore a son whom she called Alexander, 'whoever his father may have been'.

North of Dir and bounded on the west and the north by Afghanistan and the Hindu Kush is Chitral, which delights its admirers above all for the views it provides of Tirichmir — at 25,230 ft the highest peak in the Hindu Kush. Tirichmir shuts the valley off from the narrow Wakhan Corridor in Afghanistan that separates Pakistan from the Pamir Plateau and the Soviet Union.

The mountains of the 800-kilometre-long Hindu Kush — called by the Greeks 'paropanisadae' (higher than an eagle's ceiling) — are lower, but in some ways more feared than the Himalaya and the Karakorams. They have been called the Hindu Killer. The seventh-century Chinese explorer Hsuang Tsang, who journeyed through them *en route* to Swat said that when visibility was not down to zero because of swirling snow, it was down to zero because of frozen cloud.

Other travellers comment on the mountains' vastness, their silence, their eternal snow; on the wild torrents born of glaciers, the cruel precipices and the desolation of the valleys.

Left: Kalash youngster in the Chitral Valley.

Left: Young Kalash children attending a celebration.

Right: Traditional Kalash dancers celebrate one of the pagan community's many colourful festivals. Numbering fewer than 3,000, the Kalash, whose background is shrouded in mystery, are the only non-Muslim group in Chitral Valley.

In fact, there is a fascinating contrast in Chitral between the stubborn, sprawled, rugged, almost overbearing massiveness of the brown-sloped, white-topped mountains and the fragile, cropped terraces laid out below them, by which the inhabitants live.

Like the other northern valleys Chitral, long and narrow, is big with grandeur and sparing of subsistence soil. The villagers crop every inch that offers, clothing the lower slopes — according to the season and depending on the altitude and aspect — with neatly efficient terraces of wheat and maize, barley and pulses, rice and millet, and a variety of fruits: peaches, apricots, almonds and grapes. There's a sturdy cottage industry of silk-farming too. The silkworms are reared on mulberry leaves and the product sent south to Swat, where silk fabrics are manufactured.

A major attraction in Chitral are the three remote Kalash valleys — home of the non-Muslim Kafir Kalash (Black Infidels). The name refers to the extremely colourful black dress — featuring headgear covered with cowrie shells and dyed feathers — worn by the women. The men, too, wear distinctive hats, decorated with feathers or bells.

The Kafir Kalash are considered by some to be Indo-European and are consequently believed by others to be descended from Alexander the Great's men. They number fewer than 3,000 in Pakistan — there are many more in Afghanistan — and they live in rough-hewn timber houses in the beautiful, lush valleys of Bumburet, Rambur and Birir.

The distinctive music and dancing of the Kafir Kalash, together with drinking, feasting and sacrifice of goats on wooden altars, play an important part in their lively annual festivals.

Their temples are often elaborately carved, as are some of their coffins, which are not buried but left above ground. The Kafir religion seems to be little understood by others. It embraces many gods and involves the use of fire, and idol and ancestor worship.

The people of Chitral have a reputation for hospitality. They are of mixed race and, with the famous exception of the Kafir Kalash, are all Muslim. About a quarter of the population are Ismailis (followers of the Aga Khan). It is they who cultivate the grapes.

Chitralis are immensely proud of their beautiful, remote valley. Their folklore tells of a traveller who wandered into it at the end of a long journey. Wearily he sank down to rest by a stream on green velvet grass, and lying there saw reflected all kinds of luscious fruits: mulberries, apples, pears, grapes, cherries, and in the stream, ice. Hungry he ate his fill, tired he slept. When he got home he started to tell his friends at the mosque all about Chitral. But the mullah stopped him. He feared people would think the traveller had returned from Paradise.

Above: Perched atop the Murree Hills at Bhurban, Pakistan's most modern and luxurious hotel — the Pearl-Continental Hotel — commands breathtaking vistas of the rolling hills of the Kashmir Valley.

Opposite: Hill resort of Nathiagali in the Murree foothills of the scenic Pir Panjal mountains.

Like the great spiralling arms of a space galaxy three of earth's most stupendous mountain ranges stake out their claims to a place on the summit of the world. From Burma and Nepal in the southeast the supreme Himalaya run north-west for 3,000 kilometres to where the Hindu Kush start their swing down west and south-west along the border with Afghanistan, while to the north, but astonishingly near and in parallel with the Himalaya, the Karakoram march off south-eastwards and mark the border with China.

Where these mighty ranges meet they convene the densest assembly of supreme peaks on earth: eighty-two of them more than 23,000 feet high including, in one awesome twenty-five kilometre arc, ten of earth's thirty highest mountains — one of them, K2, second only to Everest.

The country is much admired by mountaineers — though heights like these are not for the inexperienced. Many lives have been lost on Pakistan's mountain slopes and ridges — counted by many professionals the most challenging anywhere in the world. Many of the peaks have never been conquered; not for want of trying, but because they have proved too difficult even for the most painstakingly prepared expeditions equipped with the most sophisticated mountaineering tackle.

Stupendous as are these heights, and formidable the extremes of weather that belong with them, they are by no means the only hazards of this forbidding country. The most terrible glaciers outside the polar regions are here to take the unwary; rockslides and avalanches are a daily occurrence. 'Karakoram' is in fact a Turkish word that means 'crumbling rock' — an ominously apt name for a range which, like its neighbour the Himalaya, is young (at fifty-five million years the youngest on earth) and thrusting relentlessly into the resisting Asian land mass — growing higher in the process — and creating earth tremors at an average of one every three minutes.

Such is Pakistan's north: a fearsome, generally impenetrable region, only ever attempted through all the centuries by the most determined, foolhardy or adventurous.

After winning Independence modern Pakistan resolved that this North must become part of the new country in reality — not just on a map; that these chillingly remote and inaccessible regions must be brought within physical reach of the rest, so that they too might share in, and contribute to the country's growth; that this North, in fact, must be opened up. To achieve this it was decided to build a road through it.

The almost outrageous enormity of the undertaking was matched by only one thing: the setting. For the idea was nothing less than to drive 850 kilometres of metalled surface, of twentieth century two-way highway capable of carrying cars, buses, and modern heavy freight vehicles from ninety-six kilometres north of the country's capital, Islamabad,through this jungle of mountains — notoriously dangerous for over 2,000 years even to set foot in — all the way to its fantastic destination, under the roof of the world, at the gates of China.

Twelve drama-packed years after it was begun the outrageous was achieved. Today the Karakoram Highway (KKH) is one of the wonders of the modern world.

Begun officially on 30 October 1966 under a 1966 Sino-Pakistan

Above: Young street food vendor in Gilgit town.

Previous pages: Summertime in the stunning grandeur of the Baltoro Glacier where, in the background, the 25,660-foot peak of Masherbrum dominates the horizon.

Above: Fruit trees blossom in an orchard in the shadow of 25,550 foot Rakaposhi.

agreement, the highway that today carries traffic up more than 12,000ft in 805 kilometres — from 2,513 feet above sea level to 15,400 — was formally opened at Hunza on 3 October 1978. By then 800 tons of explosive had been detonated to cut the bed for the seven-metre-wide carriageway and thirty million cubic yards of rock and earth had been blasted out, shifted and graded. Lining the ravines to buttress road and bridges had taken 80,000 tons of cement, and all told, a staggering total of 35,000 tons of coal and 80,000 tons of other fuel and lubricants had been used.

The project was entrusted to the Pakistan Armed Forces, and in particular to the engineers of the Frontier Works Division. Actual construction, with a force of between 2,500 and 3,000 men, began simultaneously from the south and the north. C-130s of the Pakistan Air Force airlifted men from Rawalpindi into China, where the Chinese — who had a lively interest in the project because it would open a new outlet to the Middle East and beyond — transported them to Khunjerab Pass and undertook to keep them supplied.

The C-130s played a vital role throughout. They delivered supplies —

Above: Springtime in Gilgit with its verdant grain fields and lush orchards.

including the huge, dangerous cargoes of explosives. Weather was an unrelenting hazard and the risks of flying the gigantic freight-planes heavy with bulldozers, dynamite, food and other essential supplies through the frozen, fog-prone mountain valleys practically incalculable — especially since need became greatest when conditions were worst and the troops and civilian workers were cut off from other supplies by blizzards.

On the surface — weather, earthquakes, avalanches, and mudslides permitting — 1,000 trucks shuttled men and equipment up and down between the supply bases and the painfully-slowly-advancing building zones.

Eighty-five bridges and numerous tunnel cuttings had to be built along the way — each of the bridges preceded, in the building, by a Bailey slung across the gorge to keep supplies and the work moving ever forward.

Through all the centuries before the KKH was built the only traffic through these dangerous defiles had been the mule-trains of merchants and devout Buddhists who knew, and braved, this and similar routes

Above: Palace of the Mir at Aliabad in Hunza Valley.

through the mountains — the merchants bringing from China the silk that gave these perilous ways their name, together with porcelain and lacquer-work, bronze and iron, spices, furs and tea — and taking back the other way the goods they had bartered with them in market-places like those of Gandhara: especially gold, ivory and jewels.

These intrepid spirits followed trails that offered short cuts between the great caravan towns of central Asia, China and the rich markets of the subcontinent. And they left low-key but vivid accounts of what it was like to journey through passes cut by ice-swollen rivers crashing through desolate gorges: the lair of the most savage of weathers and hazardous extremes, daunting to the most experienced travellers.

'The way was difficult and rugged', wrote the Buddhist pilgrim Fa Hien after travelling this way to the shrines of Swat early in the fifth century AD. 'It ran along a bank that was exceedingly precipitous. . . . By its edge one's eyes became unsteady. There was no way forward: nowhere to place one's foot. And below were the waters of the river called the Indus.'

Not that precipices and roaring rivers, merciless extremes of weather,

or even glaciers and avalanches exhausted the dangers. The tribes along the way in their isolated valleys were fierce in both reputation and fact; and the precipices over the Indus made disposal of enemies, whether family or foreigner, whether alive or already dead, blood-chillingly uncomplicated. In some places it was the normal way of disposing of the unproductive old.

The state of the way Fa Hien travelled got no better for the next 1,450 years; though that did not stop the most determined risking their fortunes and their lives. But with the decline of the Roman Empire trade slumped and with it Silk Route traffic; not to revive till the sixteenth century when Babur established the Mughal throne and empire.

When, in the middle of the twentieth century, the Pakistan army put dynamite and pick to solid rock to blast and break, pack, level and grade a highway that would transform communications through the country's north, the way through had lost nothing of its ancient enmity. It demanded a heavy price in blood. So, in addition to the twenty years of study and planning and the twelve years of arduous physical labour by 15,000 Pakistanis and 10,000 Chinese in the most hostile of weathers, a

Above: Fierce, anything-goes polo match at Gilgit where the game was born many centuries ago.

Above: Musicians celebrate scores in a polo match with a song specially composed for each scorer.

terrible toll of almost 1,000 human lives was also exacted.

In the end, for almost every kilometre advanced a man died. There are well-laid cemeteries and special memorials to them, but undoubtedly their finest monument is the Karakoram Highway they created — a two-lane thoroughfare through regions only the bravest had previously dared enter, and culminating in the highest metalled road across an international border on earth, in the Khunjerab Pass between Pakistan and China.

That total of fatalities, incidentally, can never be final. The Karakoram is one of those human undertakings that, of its nature, is for ever a matter of life and death. Glaciers, tearing winds, fissured rock, extremes of air and ground temperature, rock falls, mudflows, and earthquake are permanent menaces. In any case, it was estimated that the highway would need twenty years to settle down after the violent blasting of the mountains during the ten years of construction.

Maintenance is thus like constant rehabilitation. Two battalions of the Frontier Works Division, headquartered at Gilgit, are stationed along the route to secure it against the effects of earthquakes and the extremes of

Left: Youngsters at Rahimabad in the Gilgit Valley carry home the harvest.

weather that must always threaten to slow or stop movement along the highway.

Yet in its first ten years of operation the KKH only once had to close for more than one day; when Batura, the longest of the glaciers, invaded the tarmac. That took three days to clear.

Between these lethal heights and the level plains of Punjab and Sind there could hardly be less in common. Yet there are links. The most significant is water — even if the rivers here are tumultuous, boisterous; there, often sluggish and far-spreading.

And following from that, something else. The traveller through Sind and Punjab finds nothing more striking than that communities are settled and grow where the waters go; and they die where the rivers dry up. In the mountains it's the same with the KKH: it follows the rivers. First is the Indus as far as Nanga Parbat — where the river moves off resolutely east and the road turns sharply north to follow, here on its second stage, the Gilgit river, almost to Gilgit town. Next the Highway accompanies the Hunza river past dazzling Rakaposhi to Nazirabad, and there picks up the Khunjerab river, which leads it to its triumphant conclusion — China.

Above: Summer's brief but glorious face clothes the fields of Nagar Valley, near Hunza, in green.

Because of their love affair with Kashmir the Mughals considered that the chief importance of Hazara — the valley of the pleasing ease of Murree and the Ghalis — was that it led them there. Nowadays Hazara is appreciated for itself; but it has, too, a much greater, new significance. It is there — at Havelian, 100 kilometres north of Islamabad — that the KKH begins, the key now to an estimated three-quarters of Pakistan's north.

The first stretch of the way — nearly forty kilometres to Mansehra via Abbottabad — uses road built originally nearly a century ago. The scenery — fertile valleys and barren, brown hills wasted by weather — gives no inkling of the drama to come.

Abbottabad is a military town, named after the first British Deputy Commissioner of the valley district, James Abbott — one of those people others instantly warmed too, and much loved by the Hazara people. The town named for him is today an important tourist centre — with easy access to Murree and the Galis and their summer cool, and breathtaking views of terraced hills and ravine-cut forests and valleys.

The former hill-station of Thandiani, recently restored to favour through the arrival of an all-weather road from Abbottabad, offers a panorama considered by some the equal of any in Pakistan. From this splendid viewpoint can be seen the Galis to the south, the snow-capped ranges of Kashmir to the east, the Kohistan and Kaghan mountains in the north-east and north, those of Swat and Chitral round to the north-west, the Hindu Kush into Afghanistan on the west, and in the south-west, over Abbottabad itself, the distant Indus.

Mansehra, nearly twenty-five kilometres from Abbottabad, stands close to another of those ancient trade-route junctions — in this case from China and Kashmir. Here, as at Shahbaz Garhi in the Vale of Peshawar, the great, good king Ashoka posted his edicts — though here unfortunately weathering has almost obliterated the script.

The British had trouble with local tribesmen in the Black Mountains to the north and were for ever sending out punitive expeditions in unsuccessful attempts to tame them.

The highway now climbs on through pine forests before dropping down to the Indus ninety-six kilometres from Mansehra. Here, at Thakot, the first of the bridges built by the Chinese is encountered. Strongly trussed by its twin suspension towers and gracefully arched in white cement, with sculpted lions and lanterns, and dressed with pastel-coloured flowers and butterflies, it gives no hint of the hundreds of Chinese workers who were killed in rock falls and accidents while the highway and its bridges were being built.

Twenty-seven kilometres beyond the bridge is Besham — half-way to Gilgit from Islamabad and favoured as an overnight stopping place. In ancient days Chinese merchants and monks travelling to Swat, Peshawar, and beyond left the Indus at this point and went on via the nearby Shangla Pass. The road is good, but as ever in this country, becomes impassable after heavy rain.

All this is Kohistan: a district flanked by Swat on the west, Hazara to the south and east, and Gilgit Agency in the north.

The scenery is superb, with numerous valleys of unsurpassed beauty; but the region is one of Pakistan's remotest and most backward — virtually isolated before the KKH was built. Steep mountains rise to 15,000 feet, leaving the few inhabitants barely enough soil for subsistence terracing. Their houses perch on spurs and ridges that seem to afford too small a platform to hold them and no access whatever.

Across the river are some old stone forts that traditionally protected the villagers and guarded their poor crops. The Chinese Buddhist Fa Hien noted that men had chiselled paths along the rocks here, 'and distributed ladders on the face of them, to the total altogether of 700. And at the bottom there was a suspension bridge of ropes by which the river was crossed at a place where the banks were 80 paces apart'.

Some fifty kilometres further is Pattan, and before it a memorial to those who died building the road.

'. . . as you drive along, tarry a little to say a short prayer for those silent brave men of the Pakistan Army who gave their lives to realise a dream, now known as the Karakoram Highway.'

Pattan stands at the edge of a small island plate of earth's surface that is trapped between the plates of the Asian continent and the Indian subcontinent; the latter relentlessly forcing its way under the floor of

Above: Harvest of wheat at remote Misghar in the far north of the Roof of the World, even now closed to tourist traffic.

Asia — raising the mountains, geologists say, two-and-a-half centimetres every four years. The result is a sometimes terrifying instability, and the army is on permanent alert for clearing rockslides.

In 1974, while the highway was being built, an earthquake killed 5,000 people, injured three times as many and practically wiped Pattan from the face of the earth. Miraculously, several hundred Chinese workers living in tents in the area escaped harm.

Little more than thirty-two kilometres beyond Pattan the road crosses the Indus at Kamila, and soon the gorge narrows so much that a ledge had to be blasted into the sheer cliff face to carry the road 1,300 feet above the river. More workers were killed along this stretch than on any other.

Fifty kilometres from Kamila the highway turns sharply eastwards, staying with the course of the Indus. Around this broad sweeping bend the river fills a wide, sand-shored basin surrounded by bare, or at best scrub-covered mountains.

Sixty-seven kilometres on is Chilas, another ancient crossroads — as the many inscriptions on the rocks testify. These writings link travellers along this southern shore of the Indus through a 2,000-year span, with drawings of warriors, leopards and deer, Buddhas and *stupas*, verses of thanksgiving for a safe journey, invocations against harm, encouragement for those coming after. Some depict elaborate scenes of festivals, sacrifice and celebration. Various languages are found, and many inscriptions are dated and tell of the writer's origins and destination.

Chilas is where the Babusar Pass connects southwards with another remote valley that cannot be described without at least one or two superlatives — the Khaghan.

The road through the Babusar used to be the main way north to Gilgit, but with the building of the KKH it is no longer maintained.

Those who know it go to Khaghan above all for two things: the peace and quiet — there's no industry here except forestry — and the excellent fishing in the rivers and on the lakes. Trout were introduced by the British and the Pakistan government has improved stocks since. For many the centrepiece of the valley is brilliant blue Saiful Muluk Lake, about seventy-two kilometres south of Chilas. The white-capped peaks of the surrounding mountains reflect in its waters and in spring carpets of flowers surround its shores. The Khaghan is steep and narrow, so that serious sportsmen and contemplatives are not much disturbed by tourist groups looking for the high drama of the great mountain *bella vistas*.

East of Chilas is desert, pitilessly hot in summer and bitterly cold in winter — at 4,000 feet little lower in altitude than the highest point of the British Isles. Barren mountains look down on it from their 16,000 foot complacency, while about the river and the road there is nothing but dead, dried mudscape featured with boulders and sand dunes. It is the most barren reach of the way to China, but even this has its awesome compensation. Nanga Parbat, the Naked Mountain — so-called because neither snow nor vegetation can get a grip on its steep slopes — is already in sight towering over the river's southern shore.

Pakistan International Airlines' daily flights from Islamabad International Airport to Gilgit and Skardu have been called the most

Above: Youngster in a mountain village carries refreshment to a visitor.

Opposite: Jets of the Pakistan Air Force fly over the majestic snow-capped peaks which dominate the south-eastern wall of Shimshal Valley above Pasu Village on the Karakoram Highway close to the Chinese border.

Right: Young Hunzakut whose folklore claims they are descendants of the armies of Alexander the Great.

dramatic scheduled flights in commercial aviation; and the ten minutes and more it takes them to pass Nanga Parbat — likened to 'flying down a roofless tunnel' — is its indescribable climax.

Major southern buttress of the Pamir Knot, westernmost anchor of the Himalaya, sixth highest mountain in the world, Nanga Parbat is as awesome in its many aspects as it is in legend. For sheer size it is virtually without equal: within a 100-kilometre radius nothing even begins to approach it. It is not a single peak — rather a massif, culminating in a 26,660 foot ice summit. The southern flank is one of the world's most terrible precipices: a sheer drop of more than five kilometres.

Apart from Everest and Annapurna, Nanga Parbat has claimed the lives of more climbers than any other — close to fifty at the last count. But that's in absolute figures. Set against the numbers who have tried, Nanga Parbat is easily the most terrible killer.

Of the fourteen peaks on earth that exceed 26,250 feet Nanga Parbat and K2 in the Karakorams are counted the most difficult. A first attempt on the Himalayan peak was made in 1895. It failed, and three men died. Six subsequent major expeditions also failed. It wasn't till 1953 — five weeks after Everest was first climbed, by Sir Edmund Hillary and Sherpa Tenzing — that 'The Killer', as mountaineers call Nanga Parbat, was climbed by an Austro-German expedition.

Above: Spring thaw frees the ski resort of Naltar Valley from winter's bondage.

Reinhold Messner, the Austrian climber who scorched a trail across mountaineering history with his three-day solo conquest of Everest without oxygen in 1980, had special reason to remember Nanga Parbat. Ten years before his Everest triumph his younger brother, Guenther, climbing down with him after reaching the summit was swept to his death by an avalanche. Reinhold himself was by then at the end of his endurance. Twice later he was to attempt Nanga Parbat solo, but each time the enormity of the challenge defeated him, before he achieved it at his third attempt.

Messner considered his heart-breaking 1970 climb up and down Nanga Parbat as a landmark in his experience. 'The Nanga Parbat Odyssey,' he wrote, 'has given me the strength to face any future hazards squarely and accept or reject them. And every single hazardous enterprise I now undertake — whether it is successful or no — is an invisible ingredient of my life, of my fate.'

Nanga Parbat is so uncompromisingly vast that it is difficult to see it. The best views are about fifty kilometres from Chilas, where the KKH again crosses the Indus. Twenty-five kilometres further, at Jaglot, the

Above: Early summer in Naltar Valley.

Indus is joined by the river Gilgit and the highway forsakes the former and goes on north with the latter, bypassing the town of Gilgit, administrative centre of the Northern Areas, forty-three kilometres further on.

For all the bustle of its bazaars — especially strong in Chinese goods — and despite the large army presence and the constant stream of traffic along the Karakoram Highway that clings to the wall of the valley across the river, dusty Gilgit, settled in its irrigated bowl of land 5,000 feet above sea-level, seems to inhabit a time warp all its own, outside the twentieth century. Encircled by lofty, barren mountains it's surrounded by tiny terraced fields and rich fruit groves and beyond them, desert.

Gilgit's a melting pot of a town: a cosmopolitan mix of Kashgaris, Tshins, Chitralis, Paktoons and Hunzakuts. Architecturally it's quite unremarkable despite its renown — unless you count a *je ne sais quoi* of the Wild West about its laid-back streets. The appearances are deceptive, though. Gilgit is alive, very active and growing fast.

Strangely little is known about its past, other than that it was an important Silk Route staging post for over 2,000 years. Before that its

Overleaf: Trekkers in Concordia, close to K-2, the world's second-highest peak.

Opposite: Summer's apricot harvest at Altit laid out to sun dry for winter's sustenance when the Hunza Valley is cut off from the rest of the world.

Above: Vacationing student at Lake Buret, Gulmit, in the upper Hunza Valley.

Opposite: Chafing wheat at Karimabad in Hunza Valley, the region which inspired James Hilton's fabled Shangri-La, where people never aged, in the land of 'Lost Horizons'.

people are said to have been fire-worshippers before becoming Buddhists, and then Hindu before they finally embraced Islam, some time after the eleventh century. Kings of Tibet ruled the area around the seventh or eighth century AD as they did neighbouring Skardu (Baltistan); successfully contending with attempts by China and Arabia to muscle in on their dominance — sometimes in alliance with Kashmir. By the time of Marco Polo the various valleys each claimed the right to tax travellers, and in a famous phrase the Venetian described the area as 'noisy with kingdoms'.

In the late nineteenth century the British, worried about Russian expansionism, set up the Gilgit Agency as an outpost of Empire, to keep the Russians at bay.

For those who have been there this British Imperial obsession with the threat from Russia over the roof of the world — heartily reciprocated as it was — is extremely funny. The idea that at the turn of the twentieth century any nation would choose to send an army into Chitral, Gilgit, Hunza or Kashmir via the Pamir Knot — where the mountains stand taller than the Alps piled on top of the Pyrenees — was finally recognised by the British themselves as unrealistic. When the Russians and the Chinese (the third 'great power' involved) saw the point too, the three of them sat down together and agreed to take the Pamirs as their point of departure for fixing the thenceforth frontiers.

As was remarked at the time: where the boundaries were set only the Pamir eagles knew. . . .

Nonetheless it didn't stop the British playing their obsessive game of keeping an eye on the Russians. They went on sending agents to Gilgit, Hunza, Kashmir, and elsewhere to 'watch the frontier', 'observe the channels of trade', and compete with the Russian presence wherever they encountered it.

Only a few decades later, in 1947, when for Partition purposes the northern areas were declared part of Kashmir (and so destined for union with India) the strongly Islamic allegiance of the people declared vehemently for Pakistan. In the absence of the troops (who were fighting in Baltistan) the band of the Gilgit Scouts went out onto the airfield and played their bagpipes as loud as they could while the Indian Air Force tried (unsuccessfully) to bomb it. An Englishman reading the story cannot help reflecting that British influence did indeed rub off on those Britain tried to rule.

In Gilgit, as elsewhere in the northern areas, polo is the most popular sport: though with rules — such as they are — which would not be considered quite orthodox outside the region. (They certainly would not be counted 'cricket' anywhere). Noise is an essential ingredient of the game — the band playing a vital part with musical messages of encouragement, dissatisfaction and dismay understood by the enthusiastic crowds.

For visitors, trekking is the supreme activity, closely followed by fishing. But both call for experience: the trout are said to be uncommonly canny.

For those too young to have to bother with the burden of experience there are plenty of easy walks — delightful through the cultivated fields, the fruit and nut orchards, and the feed pastures beyond.

Left: Fort in remote Misghar Valley, built during World War II, and now a mountain warfare school.

The prime 'local' expedition is to the Buddha rock carving at Kargah Nullah, five or six miles from Gilgit on the road to Punial. The ten-foot figure was carved into the rock 160 feet above the ground in the seventh century AD. In 1934 the so-called 'Gilgit manuscripts' — Buddhist texts dating from the same period as the carving — were found amid the remains of three *stupas* that can still be seen less than a kilometre upstream.

Further on still — 10,000 feet high and surrounded by snow-topped mountains — is Naltar, beautiful itself, and a good centre for forest walks and fishing expeditions.

At Gilgit the Karakoram Highway has now reached what is generally agreed to be its most spectacular and stunningly beautiful section — the 210-kilometre passage, much of it along the river Hunza, to Sost. Before re-embarking on this road and completing the journey to Kunjerab, it should be noted that the Indus has turned east into the area called Baltistan — also known, from its capital, as Skardu. Once again the highway — or in this case an offshoot of it that follows the Indus, while the main road carries on north beside the Hunza river — has opened a vast area formerly isolated and reached only by the determined few. This amazing 'side-road' puts the most easterly reach of the northern territories in touch with the rest of the country and makes Concordia, the Cathedrals, the Gasherbrums, Masherbrum, the Baltoro, and Saltoro

Above: Suspension bridge over the Indus under the Roof of the World.

Glaciers, and K2 accessible to more tourists than could previously have hoped to reach them.

Most of Baltistan, however, is high altitude desert, with little rain and correspondingly little farming — except where tributaries of the Indus provide enough soil for the typical northern narrow terracing. Hilary Adamson quotes a Swedish expert called upon in 1978 to advise on construction of the road through the Skardu plateau as saying: 'What kind of mountains are these! There is no vegetation, no trees, no grass, no water, no birds, only miles and miles of black rock. Huge boulders of black rock come hurtling down from the top without ever having been disturbed.' The expert reckoned it was better to forget about building a road there.

Because of its mainly barren character, interspersed with lush valleys, the territory is commonly nicknamed 'Little Tibet'. In fact in a number of respects the Balti life-style reflects that of Tibetans, who were at one time politically dominant in this region. The inhabitants still speak an archaic dialect of the Tibetan language: and it is certain that they were Buddhist before they were converted to Islam.

Above: The lake resort of Shangri-La in Skardu Valley under the spread of Nanga Parbat — the 'Naked Mountain'.

Opposite: Crystal pure water from a mountain spring gushes along its bed in Misghar Valley, ancient gateway to the Silk Route.

On the other hand there is no truth in the tale that Alexander the Great founded Skardu. It's even suggested that the name, and its alternative form Askandria, are clearly akin to the Indian version of the name Alexander, Iskander. But the truth is neither Alexander not any of his men came this far.

In 1839 Baltistan was taken over by Kashmir, and then in 1947 the Baltis found themselves subjects of an attempt to incorporate them formally into the newly independent India. Like the people of Gilgit the Baltis rebelled and opted to join Pakistan.

The region has much in common with Chitral and Hunza in the north and north-west, but is generally bleaker. Skardu itself has an interesting steep-staired fortress but otherwise little to show for itself. On the other hand it is possibly the best base in the world for trekking and mountaineering. The nearby Satpara and Kachura lakes are greatly admired for their majestic silence and, in spring, the abundance of flowers and fruit blossom. Further out are the picturesque valleys and stony gorges that lead to the most glamorous trekking country of all. The routes, of varying difficulty, include the famous Baltoro trek.

Strictly for the hardy this thirty-day expedition leaves populated areas

Opposite: Shifting sands of the Skardu Valley, a replica of the Sahara in the high frozen mountains of Pakistan's Roof of the World.

Left: Youngsters in Shimshal Village, under the Roof of the World, live at the edge of existence earning respite only during the brief warmth of summer.

after three days and passes by way of rugged gorges, moraines and glaciers to Concordia, where the Baltoro unites ten of the world's top thirty peaks. They include Masherbrum,25,660 feet, Broad Peak, 26,400 feet, Hidden Peak (Gasherbrum 1), 26,470 feet and K2, 28,250 feet second in height only to Mount Everest.

It has been well said that nature will not be admired by proxy. Statistics have as much to do with the majesty of mountains as the pocket calculator that pops them up. Words are struck dumb; here, indeed, great pictures are worth their thousands of words. Only a master can write adequately of such a sight — one who has been there, to the top, and knows from personal experience: like Kurt Diemberger who conquered Broad Peak (for the second time that day, in his case) with the veteran Hermann Buhl. They arrived there dangerously late, as the sun was going down:

'Now was the moment of ineffable truth — the silence of space around us, ourselves silent. This was utter fulfilment. The sun bent trembling to the horizon. Down there was the night, and under it the world. Only up here, and for us, was there light. Close over yonder the Gasherbrum summits glistened in all their magic. Straight ahead, against the last light, K2 reared its dark and massive head. Soft as velvet, all colours merging into a single dark gleam. The snow was suffused with a deep orange tint, while the sky was a remarkable azure. As I looked out, an enormous

Opposite: Bleached, eroded and forbidding, the Shimshal Pass is inhospitable in summer and impassable in winter.

Right: Early spring brings promise of welcome warmth to these children of Khaplu Village, in the Shyok Valley, in the shadow of the Masherbrum mountain range.

pyramid of darkness projected itself over the limitless wastes of Tibet, to lose itself in the haze of impalpable distance — the shadow of Broad Peak. There we stood, speechless, and shook hands in silence. . . .'

Only another kind of master, a poet, could approach that — a Gerard Manley Hopkins; as when, seeing the precariousness of all being in terms of mountain heights he wrote:

'O the mind, mind has mountains, cliffs of fall
Frightful, sheer, no-man-fathomed. Hold them cheap
May who ne'er hung there. . . .'

Here is the might and the terror and the wonder of such an arena as Concordia. It makes us aware of the sharp edge of being: and clinging to its precarious slopes poor man is overwhelmed with wonder.

From Gilgit there are two ways back onto the Karakoram Highway, now travelling north on the eastern side of the Hunza river. The shorter way is over Asia's longest suspension bridge, which crosses the Hunza river near the confluence with the Gilgit. The main road joins KKH lower, on the south bank of the Gilgit, before it crosses to the eastern side of the Hunza.

Opposite: Thousand-year-old Altit Fort in the Hunza Valley.

The Gilgit bridge was erected by the Chinese and like others is stylishly distinguished by typically Chinese ornament — in this case by tigers carved into the structure.

The Chinese lost in the building of the highway were buried in the cemetery above the bridge, in the shade of trees and surrounded by the mountains they helped to build a way through.

The first settlements after Gilgit are on the western side of the Hunza. Thirty-two kilometres upriver is Nomal — and a memorial to those who died building the highway — and then Chalt, where a different kind of sign draws attention to the geology of the area. 'Here two continents collide', it states. You are in fact now leaving the island slab you have been travelling over since Pattan, and moving onto the Asian continental plate. But between Nomal and Chalt the way is rugged indeed.

This is the way to fabled Hunza where (according to the fables) all is brotherly (and, one supposes, sisterly) love; where peace and justice and respect for the environment reign; where nobody dies before his or her 120th birthday.

The catch is the road that leads there — almost literally a dark night of the flesh, for the gorge is so narrow, and thousands of feet sheer and practically vertical. Three hours is as long as the sun itself can get a look in. Modern travellers — blessed with the Karakoram tarmac that does it all for them — cannot but wonder how it was possible for ancient Silk Route man to get through himself, let alone see his pack animals through; and all their baggage.

Frequently of course Silk Route man did not get through — or reached his destination without his four-footed fortune.

The road, like the river, has been skirting the northern flanks of what for many is the loveliest of all the stupendously beautiful mountains of Pakistan's north; and here at Chalt it become visible: the superb 25,550-foot triangular-ridged Rakaposhi — towering, snow-covered and magnificent — the southernmost peak of the Karakorams.

Rakaposhi dominates the ancient south bank kingdom of Nagar, once one with the former kingdom of Hunza on the northern side of the river but for centuries — since, it is said, a bitter feud between brothers — traditional enemies. For about nineteen kilometres the KKH runs through Nagar territory before crossing the river to Hunza at Nazirabad. Eight or nine kilometres beyond that the road turns a corner and discovers Hunza proper.

Today's traveller may well feel that after so many gorges barren of everything but danger this idyllic valley must have erased, if only briefly, all discontent from the wearied merchants who perhaps had lost everything but their own lives in the grim gorges that discouraged their approach.

Still today the immense grandeur of the high valley walls is dressed, virtually to the snowline, with neat fans of river-laid soil, diligently terraced with high stone walls and trees, and sown with a succession of crops that seem chosen for the variety of their seasonally changing colours — greens, golds, and ochres.

Society in this *Shangri-la* shows remarkably little range in personal wealth. Each family grows enough fruit, nuts and grain for its own use.

Opposite: Ancient rock carving at Ganesh in the Hunza Valley.

Fruit is still the staple diet, but changes in this, as in life generally, are resulting from the increase in contact with the outside world brought by the Karakoram Highway. Nevertheless the fable of carefree industry here reaping the reward of happy, assured advanced old-age for all, is a fable. Many do live long, and disciplined living here as elsewhere breeds happiness in the people. But life is hard in Hunza and infant mortality is still high.

The 30,000 people of the ancient kingdom have been ruled by the same family for most of 1,000 years. Almost inevitably, it seems, it is claimed that Hunzakuts are descended from a party of soldiers from the army of Alexander the Great who wandered this way. It is a fact that here — as in a number of valleys in north Pakistan — fair skins and green or blue eyes in some of the inhabitants betoken the admixture of outside blood at some time in the people's past; but there is no other evidence to support the link with Alexander the Great or his men. The language spoken in central Hunza seems unrelated to any other. In the higher valley the tongue is similar to that spoken in China's Xinjiang region.

Hunza, like Gilgit was always an important staging post on the Silk Route, and profited from raids on caravans and neighbours — not disdaining a trade in slaves. Its remoteness kept it free of British interference till 1874.

Karimabad, the old capital of the kingdom, offers access to the two outrageously-daringly built forts of Baltit and Altit.

From its hilltop perch at the entrance to Ultar Gorge, Baltit Fort looks out over the entire valley: itself overlooked and made almost insignificant by the vast sprawling bulk of 24,240 foot Ultar mountain. Tibetan influence in this 400-year-old residence — occupied until 1960 — is easy to see. It's an intriguing place: rambling through more than fifty rooms on three floors. They include guest-rooms and guard rooms, prisons, stores, a throne room, quarters for the Queen Mother and an arms depot. The museum room contains the drums that were sounded to warn of enemy attack. From the roof there is a fine view of Rakaposhi. The whole area offers stunning views of mountains, glaciers and chasmic drops into ravines.

Just over a kilometre away is the yet more exciting Altit Fort — set upon a rock with a sheer 1,000-foot drop to the Hunza river. It's 100 years older than Baltit, but otherwise like it in size and layout. Murder was done here about the turn of the century in a struggle for power between brothers.

Also reached from Karimabad is the historically intriguing village of Ganesh, in a bend of the Hunza river further upstream. Carvings and inscriptions on rocks outside the village are between 1,500 and 2,000 years old, with references to Gondophares — Kushan king of Gandhara in the first century AD — and Chandragupta II, most powerful of the Mauryan kings, who ruled India early in the fifth century. There are many drawings of hunting scenes — most of them featuring the ibex, which, interestingly, still features in festivals in remote parts of Hunza nowadays.

At Ganesh the Karakoram is at its most spectacular — perched high on the eastern side of the river but dominated by half a dozen peaks

Below: Baltoro Glacier descending from Concordia,
the centrestage of the Roof of the World.

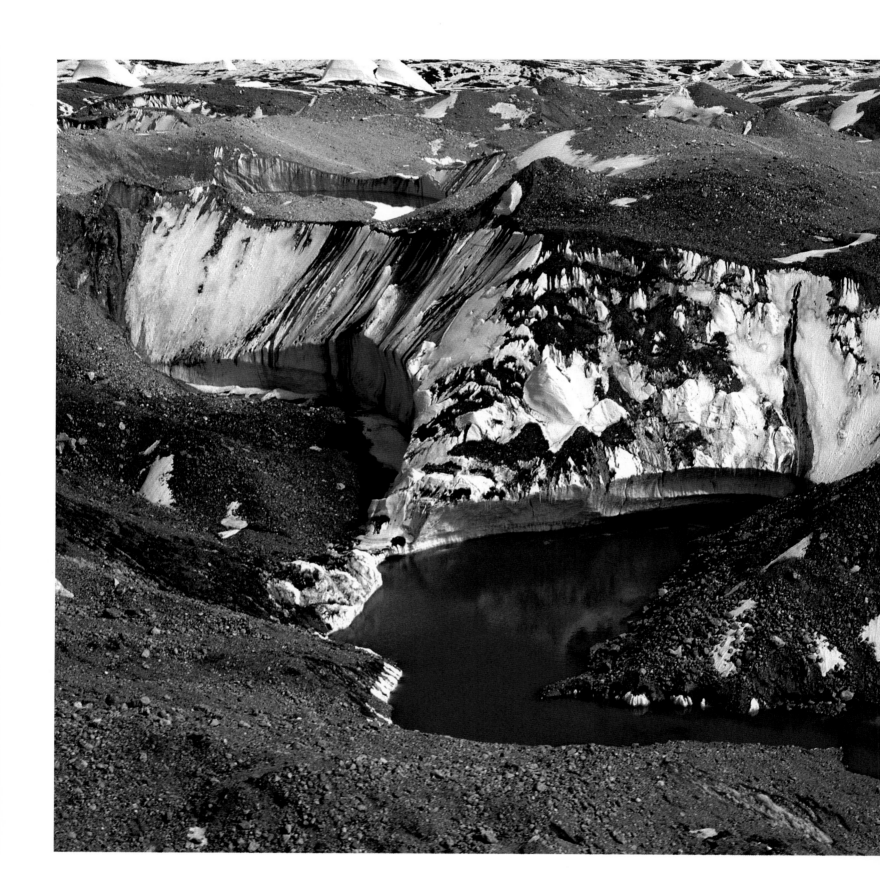

soaring over 23,000 feet. On the other side of the river is Ultar mountain, bearing limpet-like clusters of dwellings on its sides.

Then at Shishkot Bridge the highway crosses to the western side again, and not far beyond is Gulmit amid fabulous views of mountains. You are now halfway between Gilgit and the border with China. Glaciers visit the roadside here — notably Passu, classically white and ridged the way a glacier should be. Above it half a dozen more of the numberless peaks top 25,000 feet, and on the other side of the river it's the same. The mind gropes for wonder enough, and prays for memory to hold what defies expression.

Passu is another important mountain-climbing and trekking centre, offering expeditions to the Batura, Passu, Lupgar and Kuk peaks and treks up the Shimshal Valley and Batura glacier.

Thirty-two kilometres on is Sost, and a Pakistan Immigration and Customs post, eighty kilometres inside the border.

Less spectacular now, the road abandons the Hunza river to follow the Khunjerab — which itself soon dwindles to stream proportions that suggest nothing of the torrents that will quickly gather force from confluence with hundreds of other such seemingly negligible watercourses off the surrounding heights.

After the checkpost at Dih the highway hairpins up to the pass itself — at 15,528 feet the highest metal road international border crossing on earth. Thirty-two kilometres on is Pirali, the Chinese border post, and an astonishingly different world. Pakistan, at the end, was all desert gorges and vertical ranges of peaks — a no-man's land for half the way since Sost. But China here is green, wide open, grassy, with herds of yaks and sheep and goats, and children and dogs playing among the ancient Mongol-style *yurt* tents.

The international significance of the KKH, linking Pakistan with China and providing China with another route to the west, is obvious — but impossible to quantify. Within Pakistan too, its importance for trade and regional development is clear — although statistics cannot usefully be cited, since almost any development in the marketing of fruit or handicrafts, for example, is an advance on the virtually non-existent trade of the years before the highway was built.

Official sources offer some help. They say the increased availability of goods in Pakistan's North resulting from the road link with the capital region has brought prices down to one-third of their pre-1978 levels. Both incomes and standards of living, they say, have risen.

That's surely the case. The apples, pears, peaches, and apricots grown here were always rated the equal of any in the world, but before the KKH was built much of it wasted or was given away. Today northern fruit farmers are guaranteed reliable markets throughout the country. Tourism likewise has grown enormously and with it the handicrafts market.

Side by side with these economic improvements have come new schools, clinics, telephones, and other telecommunications systems.

Opposite: Biafo Glacier streams eastward almost sixty kilometres and is linked head to head with the westward flowing Hispar Glacier which stretches more than sixty kilometres.

Below: Snout of the aptly-named Tong Glacier close to Baltoro Glacier on the way to K-2.

And the existence of the KKH makes easier and encourages more road-building in this once virtually unknown and consequently neglected region. Several other link projects in the area have already been started.

Built with twentieth-century skills in defiance of ages-old hazards and kept daily operational despite ever-present danger, the Karakoram Highway is undoubtedly one of the most daring undertakings and triumphant achievements of the modern world. As such it is the perfect symbol of the twentieth century young, thousands of years old, ever ancient and ever-new Pakistan.

Overleaf: Rugged beauty of Mustagh II. At 25,361 feet, Pakistan's sixteenth highest and the world's thirty-fifth highest mountain towers over the scree, rubble and ice of Batura Glacier in the Roof of the World.

Following pages: Masherbrum rises 25,660 feet into the sky above the Yermanendu Glacier.

Pages 254-255: The jet stream sends a continuous plume of spindrift trailing westwards from the 28,250-feet-high pyramid summit of K-2, the second-highest point on earth as Pakistan Air Force jets sweep by its midriff.

Page 256: F16s of the Pakistan Air Force keep constant vigil day and night in their defence of Pakistan and the sovereignty of its skies.

الرحمٰن الرحيم

محمد

يوم الدين إياك نعبد وإياك نستعين

أنعمت عليهم

الضالين